Editor in Chief • PHILLIP BACON

Professor of Geography
Teachers College, Columbia University

Managing Editor • JOANNA ALDENDORFF

Picture Researcher • PETER J. GALLAGHER

Associate Editor • PETER R. LIMBURG

Cartographer • VINCENT KOTSCHAR

Picture Editor • ROBERT J. GARLOCK

Designer • FRANCES GIANNONI

Staff • JUDY KORMAN, BARBARA VINSON, KATHLEEN SEAGRAVES, JOHANNA GREENWALD

Special Section of Statistical Maps • RICHARD EDES HARRISON

Covers • RAY PIOCH

Complete List of Books

These books tell the exciting story of how people live in all parts of the world. You will see how men use the land for farming and industry. You will learn about mountains and deserts, oceans and rivers, cities and towns—and you will discover how the daily life of people in other countries compares with your own.

BOOK 1 • NORTH AMERICA

BOOK 2 • SOUTH AMERICA

BOOK 3 • EUROPE

BOOK 4 • ASIA

BOOK 5 • AFRICA

BOOK 6 • AUSTRALIA, OCEANIA
AND THE POLAR LANDS

WITH A SPECIAL SECTION OF
STATISTICAL MAPS AND INDEX

BOOK 1

NORTH AMERICA

BY PHILLIP BACON

*Professor of Geography,
Teachers College, Columbia University*

THE GOLDEN BOOK

PICTURE ATLAS

OF THE WORLD

IN SIX VOLUMES

Illustrated with More than 1,000 Color Photographs and Maps

GOLDEN PRESS · NEW YORK

© COPYRIGHT 1960 BY GOLDEN PRESS, INC. DESIGNED AND PRODUCED BY ARTISTS AND WRITERS PRESS, INC. PRINTED IN THE U.S.A. BY WESTERN PRINTING AND LITHOGRAPHING COMPANY. PUBLISHED BY GOLDEN PRESS, INC., ROCKEFELLER CENTER, NEW YORK 20, N. Y.

Surf from the Atlantic Ocean washes Maine's rock-rimmed coast.

THIS IS NORTH AMERICA

North America is a huge continent. Only Asia and Africa are larger. And only two other continents have more people. These two continents are Asia and Europe. Today more than 250 million people share the land of North America.

Even though North America is smaller in size and population than some other continents, its people have made great progress. This seems especially true when you learn that fewer than nine out of every 100 persons in the world live in North America. North America is still a young continent insofar as people are concerned.

North America's first settlers were the ancestors of the Indians. They came from Asia, across the Bering Strait, many thousands of years ago. By the time the first white men sailed westward from Europe and discovered North America, Indian peoples had spread across the continent. But even after so many years, the Indians were still few in number.

With the coming of Europeans, North America's population began to grow rapidly. In time, people from every part of the world came to North America. They came to find new homes and new opportunities in this "New World."

As the people from the Old World occupied North America, they tried to find those places best suited to their ways of life. Many choices lay open to them. From the islands of the Arctic Ocean to the tropical waters of the Caribbean Sea, almost every kind of climate and landform could be found in North America.

The newcomers landed on a variety of coasts, from sandy plains to rocky cliffs. Inland they found rolling hills and fertile valleys. Beyond the hills rose mountains, some old and worn-down, with forests cov-

NORTH AMERICA

Scale 1:30,000,000

0 100 200 300 400 500 Miles

NEW YORK   Cities over   1,000,000 population
Milwaukee   Cities of 250,000 — 1,000,000 population
Galveston   Cities under   250,000 population
⊕ Capitals of Countries

Depths in feet:
over 650   0–650

Heights in feet:
Below sea level   0–650   650–1650   1650–4900   over 4900

Arid Regions   Tundra   Swamp, marsh   — Railroads   ·· Canals   ⌁ Head of navigation   ↟ Falls

Oceans and Seas

ARCTIC OCEAN
PACIFIC OCEAN
ATLANTIC OCEAN
Beaufort Sea
Chukchi Sea
Bering Strait
Baffin Bay
Hudson Bay
Hudson Strait
Davis Strait
Denmark Strait
Gulf of Alaska
Gulf of Mexico
Gulf of Campeche
Gulf of Tehuantepec
Gulf of California
Gulf of Darien
Caribbean Sea
Sargasso Sea
Chesapeake Bay
Delaware Bay
Labrador Sea

Place Names

North Pole
Asia
U.S.S.R.
Kolyma Range
Kolyma
Anadyr Range
Kamchatka
Gulf of Anadyr
Bear Is.
Wrangel I.
Point Barrow
Cape Bathurst
St. Lawrence I.
Nome
ALASKA
Alaska Range
Fairbanks
Anchorage
Brooks Range
Yukon
Alaska Penins.
Kodiak I.
Mt. St. Elias
Mt. Logan 19850
Mt. Columbia 12290
Whitehorse
Juneau
Alexander Arch.
Queen Charlotte Is.
Vancouver I.
Vancouver
Seattle
Mt. Rainier
Columbia River
Portland
Mt. Hood
Mt. Shasta
Oakland
San Francisco
Yosemite Nat. Park
Sierra Nevada
Mt. Whitney 14495
LOS ANGELES
Guadalupe I. (Mex.)
Clarion I.
Socorro I.
Revilla Gigedo Is.
Clipperton I.
Cocos I. (Costa Rica)

CANADA
British Columbia
Alberta
Saskatchewan
Manitoba
Edmonton
Calgary
Regina
Winnipeg
Lake Winnipeg
Great Bear Lake
Great Slave Lake
Lake Athabaska
Reindeer Lake
Lesser Slave Lake
Yellowknife
Ft. Simpson
Ft. Nelson
Port Radium
Northwest Territories
Coppermine
Victoria I.
Banks I.
Melville I.
Prince of Wales
Boothia Peninsula
Melville Pen.
Parry Islands
Sverdrup Islands
Devon
Baffin Island
Southampton I.
Churchill
Port Nelson
Fort Hope
Knob Lake
Goose Bay
Labrador (Nfld.)
Nain
Hebron
Quebec
MONTREAL
Ottawa
TORONTO
Lake Ontario
Lake Erie
Lake Huron
Lake Superior
Lake Michigan
Sudbury
Fort William
Port Arthur
New Brunswick
Prince Edward I.
St. John
Nova Scotia
Halifax
Cape Breton I.
Newfoundland
St. John's
Gander
Cape Race
Anticosti I.

Greenland / North Atlantic

GREENLAND
Thule
Etah
Upernavik
Godhavn
Sondre Stromfjord
Holsteinsborg
Godthaab
Julianehaab
Angmagssalik
Cape Farewell
Jan Mayen (Norway)
ICELAND
Reykjavik
Faeroe Is. (Den.)
Scandinavia
Norway
Arctic Circle
Bermuda Islands (Br.)

United States

UNITED STATES
Rocky Mountains
Great Basin
Great Salt Lake
Salt Lake City
Yellowstone Park
Columbia Plateau
Colorado Plateau
Bitterroot Range
Wasatch Mts.
Black Hills
Badlands
Denver
Pikes Peak
Mt. Elbert 14431
Santa Fe
Albuquerque
El Paso
Dallas
Houston
San Antonio
Galveston
Omaha
Kansas City
St. Louis
Minneapolis
St. Paul
Milwaukee
CHICAGO
DETROIT
Cleveland
Cincinnati
Pittsburgh
Buffalo
Niagara Falls
Baltimore
Washington D.C.
PHILADELPHIA
NEW YORK
Boston
Cape Cod
Long Island
Appalachian Mts.
Allegheny Mts.
Ozark Mts.
Atlanta
Birmingham
Charleston
Savannah
Jacksonville
New Orleans
Miami
Mt. Mitchell 6684
Cape Hatteras
Mississippi R.
Missouri R.
Red River
Rio Grande
Arkansas R.
Ohio R.
Canadian R.
Gulf Stream

Mexico and Central America

MEXICO
MEXICO CITY
Monterrey
Tampico
Mazatlan
Guadalajara
Acapulco
Vera Cruz
Merida
Yucatan
Sierra Madre
Baja California
Popocatepetl 17883
Orizaba 18700
Nevado de Colima
Jorullo
Paricutin
GUATEMALA
Guatemala
BRITISH HONDURAS
Belize
HONDURAS
Tegucigalpa
EL SALVADOR
San Salvador
NICARAGUA
Managua
Lake Nicaragua
COSTA RICA
San Jose
PANAMA
Panama
Colon
Gulf of Panama

West Indies

CUBA
Havana
Santiago de Cuba
JAMAICA (W.I.)
HAITI
DOMINICAN REPUBLIC
Hispaniola
Port-au-Prince
Ciudad Trujillo
PUERTO RICO
Bahama Is. (Br.)
Great Antilles
Florida Strait
Yucatan Channel
Windward Passage

South America

COLOMBIA
Bogotá
Medellín
Barranquilla
Cali
Pasto
ECUADOR
Quito
Equator
Tropic of Cancer

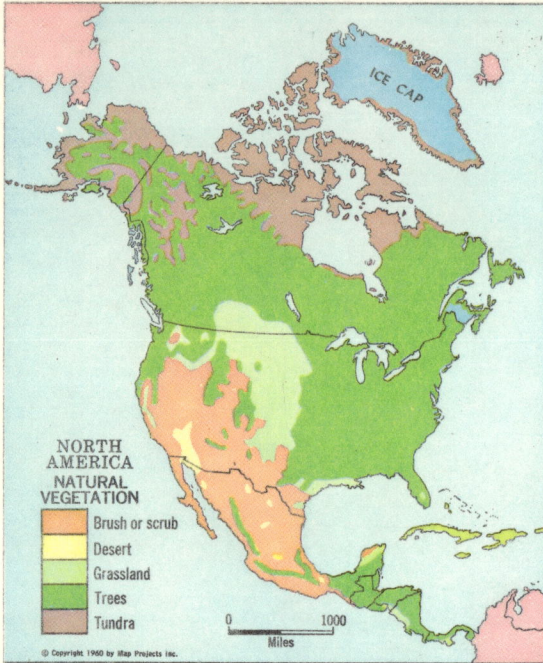

NORTH
AMERICA
NATURAL
VEGETATION

Brush or scrub
Desert
Grassland
Trees
Tundra

0   1000
Miles

© Copyright 1960 by iMap Projects Inc.

Farm buildings, fields, and highways on the level prairies of the North American Midwest form neat checkerboard patterns when seen from the air.

where the land was higher and drier, the plains were covered with a carpet of short grass, over which the mighty herds of buffalo roamed. There were deserts waiting for men to bring water to make the dry sands burst into bloom. Tropical rain-forests covered the warm, wet regions to the south, and far to the north lay the frozen tundra, home of the musk ox and the caribou.

People from northern Europe found the same kinds of trees and wild animals in eastern Canada and the United States that they had known at home. And people from Spain found in Mexico and the southwestern United States a region much like their own southern European homeland.

Almost all of the crops grown in the Old World did well in the New World. People from northern Europe brought their grains,

ering their slopes, and others young and rugged, with barren, rocky peaks. In the great central basin of the continent lay the prairie, deep in long grass. Further west,

This is desert country in the southwestern United States. Navajo Indians graze their flocks of sheep and goats on these dry pastures.

Royal Lowy—American Indian Archives

The forested slopes of Vermont's Green Mountains shelter this tiny village. The white spire of the village church is a familiar landmark.

Winston Pote—Shostal

USDA

In Louisiana, coastal swamplands are called bayous. This bayou is filled with moss-covered cypress trees, an important source of timber.

Richard Magruder—FPG

Here is the California coast. For more than 1,000 miles the waters of the blue Pacific Ocean crash on California's shoreline.

Courtesy of TWA—Trans World Airlines

C. R. Twidale

The Laurentian Upland of Canada is a vast rock-and-water plain. Its ancient and highly mineralized rocks cover five sixths of Quebec, Ontario, and Manitoba.

Forests cover the lower slopes of the Rocky Mountains. Still higher are barren or snow-covered peaks. This mountain wall stretches from the southwestern United States northward across Canada into Alaska.

Frenec Berko—Black Star

fruit trees, vegetables, and livestock. Spaniards brought their grapevines and citrus trees. Even plants native to the Far East did well in North America. Fine crops of rice were planted in low-lying, swampy places. And sugar cane made fortunes for many a planter in Louisiana and the Caribbean islands.

As settlers pushed farther and farther west in Canada and the United States they left the forested lands behind them and entered the drier grasslands of the Great Plains. Here was a wonderful grazing land. Herds of long-horned cattle gradually replaced the buffalo, the "cattle" of the Plains Indians. Spanish settlers also opened great ranches in the drier regions of Mexico.

The Indians' food plants made a very important contribution toward helping the white man settle North America. Although many white men came to North America seeking riches in gold and furs, the Indian food plants they discovered soon proved more valuable than these. From the Indians the newcomers got many plants which are still important to every one of us.

The most important Indian food plant was corn. But the Indian also gave the white man white and sweet potatoes, tomatoes, squash, several kinds of beans, pumpkins, and many other foods. Without these, many an early settler would have starved. Soon they became important in many other parts of the world as well. Another important Indian plant was tobacco.

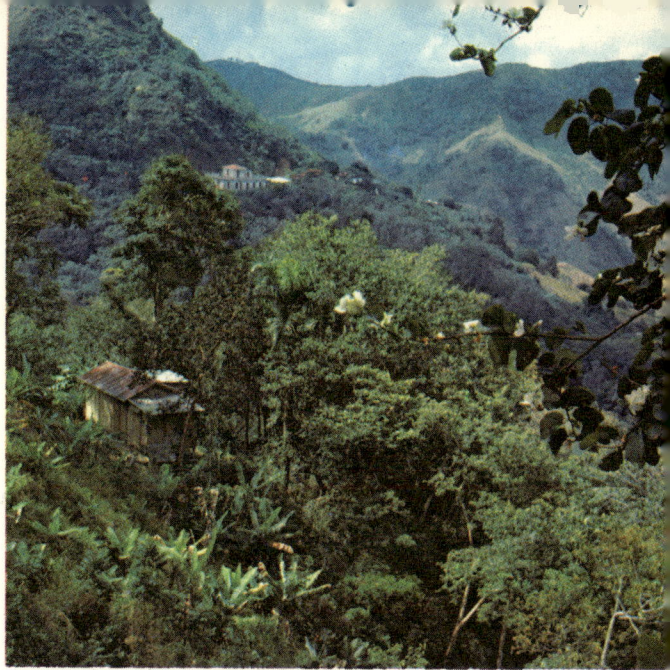

Courtesy of the Commonwealth of Puerto Rico

Year-round warm weather and plenty of rain produce dense forests like this one in Puerto Rico.

Sandy beaches, palm trees, and a warm winter sun attract thousands of tourists to Florida.

Courtesy of the Florida State News Bureau

Northern North America is covered by thousands of square miles of marshy Arctic tundra.

Rutherford Platt

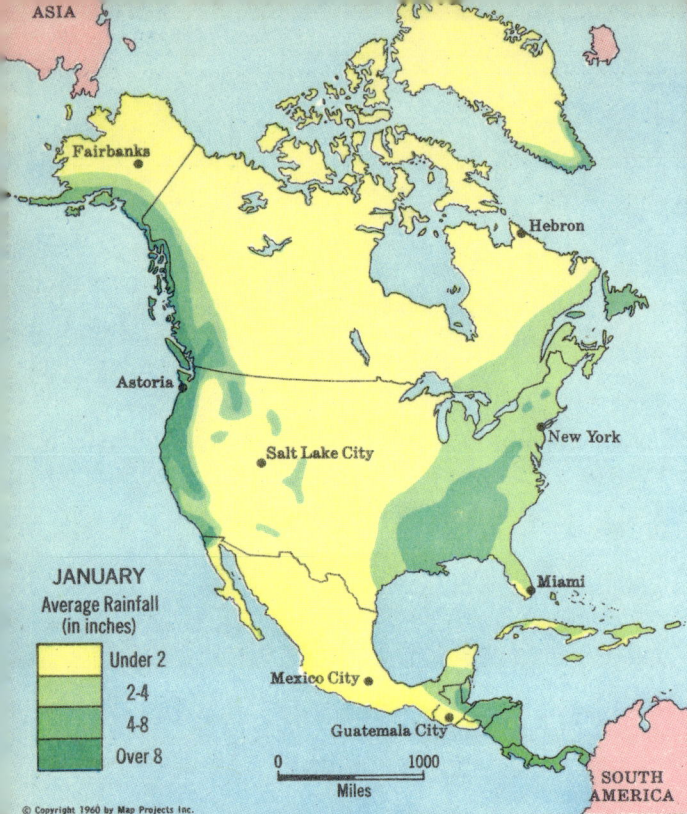

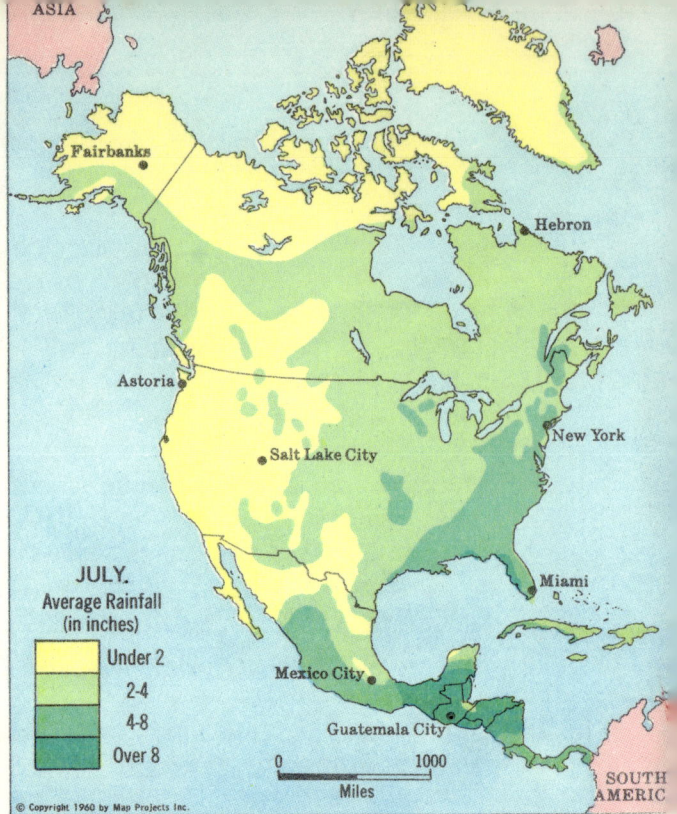

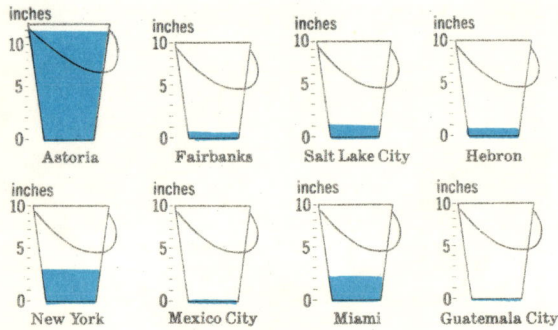

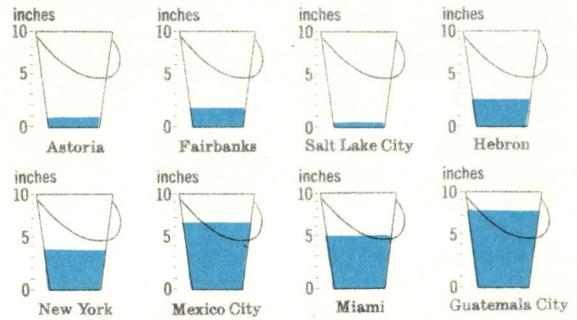

Fairbanks

Hebron

Astoria

Salt Lake City

New York

Miami

JANUARY
Average Rainfall
(in inches)

Under 2

2-4

4-8

Over 8

Mexico City

Guatemala City

0   1000
Miles

© Copyright 1960 by Map Projects Inc.

SOUTH
AMERICA

Fairbanks

Hebron

Astoria

Salt Lake City

New York

Miami

JULY
Average Rainfall
(in inches)

Under 2

2-4

4-8

Over 8

Mexico City

Guatemala City

0   1000
Miles

© Copyright 1960 by Map Projects Inc.

SOUTH
AMERIC

inches — Astoria
inches — Fairbanks
inches — Salt Lake City
inches — Hebron
inches — New York
inches — Mexico City
inches — Miami
inches — Guatemala City

inches — Astoria
inches — Fairbanks
inches — Salt Lake City
inches — Hebron
inches — New York
inches — Mexico City
inches — Miami
inches — Guatemala City

CLIMATE

If you look carefully at the maps on these two pages they will show you that North America has many climates. There are places that are warm the year around, and there are places covered with ice and snow where summer never comes. There are vast areas of parched desert land, and there are also wet places where more than 100 inches of rain fall each year.

The two temperature maps show you that the southern portions of North America are warmest. It is warm in January as well as July. This should not surprise you. These places are closest to the equator. The farther north you go, the greater are the differences between the temperatures of January and July. And the climate of places far to the north is much colder.

The United States occupies a large area in the central portion of the North American continent. Winters in the northern portion of the country are long and cold. In the South, winters are much shorter. Average temperatures in January are mild. Because the northern part of the country has such long winters, the growing season is quite short.

In the South the growing season is much longer. In fact, in some states it is nine months in length. And even farther south, in parts of Mexico and Central America, average temperatures are high every month. The growing season lasts all year.

The climate of places is affected by other

JANUARY
Average Temperature in Degrees Fahrenheit

Fairbanks

Hebron

Astoria

Salt Lake City

New York

Miami

Mexico City

Guatemala City

- Under 32
- 32-60
- 60-72
- Over 72

0   1000
Miles

SOUTH AMERICA

Copyright 1960 by Map Projects Inc.

JULY
Average Temperature in Degrees Fahrenheit

Fairbanks

Hebron

Astoria

Salt Lake City

New York

Miami

Mexico City

Guatemala City

- Under 32
- 32-60
- 60-72
- Over 72

0   1000
Miles

SOUTH AMERICA

Copyright 1960 by Map Projects Inc.

Astoria   Fairbanks   Salt Lake City   Hebron

New York   Mexico City   Miami   Guatemala City

Astoria   Fairbanks   Salt Lake City   Hebron

New York   Mexico City   Miami   Guatemala City

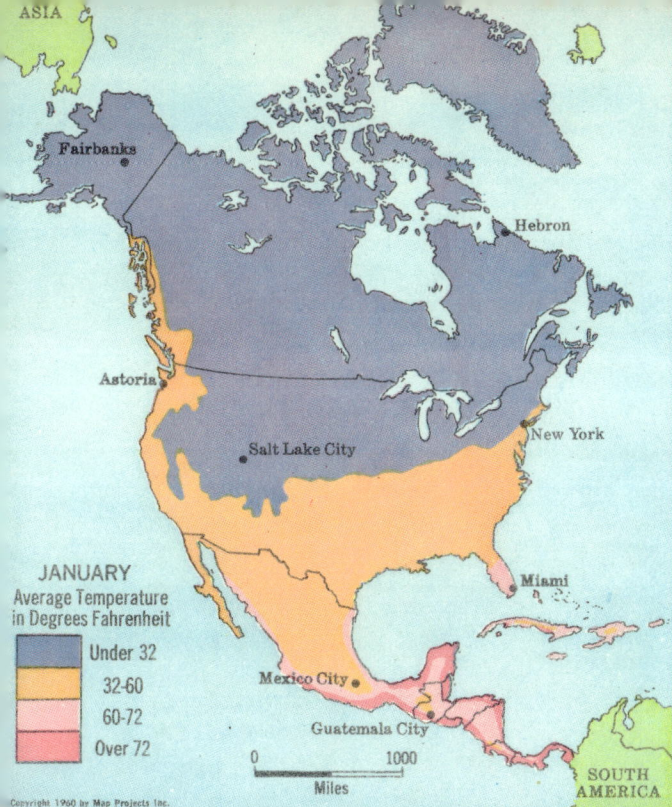

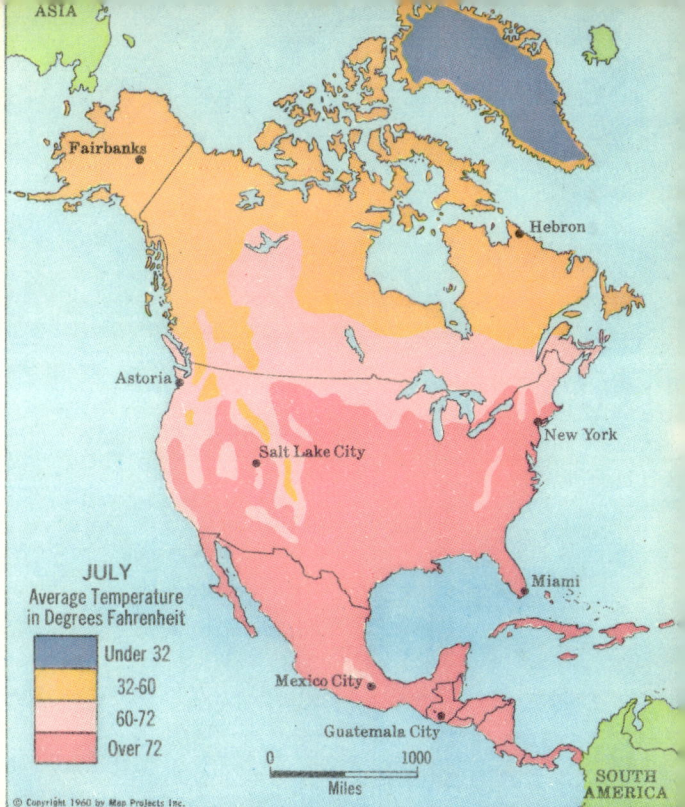

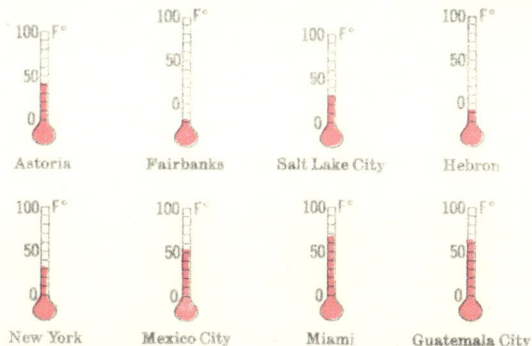

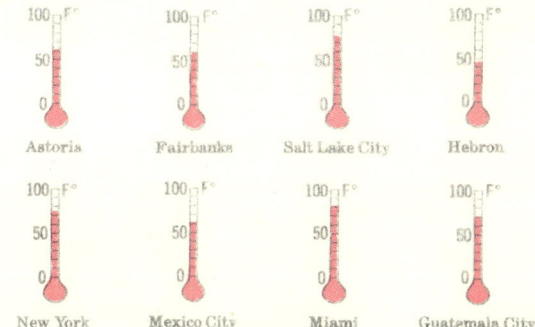

things besides distance from the equator. Landforms also affect climate. For example, a great belt of mountainous land stretches along the western edge of North America, from Alaska south to Panama. Some of these mountains are so high that snow can be seen on their peaks even in summer. Summer days are often bright and warm in the mountains, but the nights are cold. The growing season is far shorter than in the lowlands.

Oceans also affect climate. Compare temperatures along the coasts with those deep in the interior of the continent. Winters are colder in the interior than along the coasts, and summers are warmer.

Rainfall is just as important as temperature in describing the climate of places.

Look at the rainfall maps. It is plain to see that parts of the Pacific coast are very wet. The high mountains of this region are responsible for all this rain. They catch the moisture-laden air that blows in from the Pacific Ocean.

To the east, beyond the mountains, there is a vast dry region. This dry land extends from Canada to Mexico. It is far from any ocean. It has little opportunity to capture moisture from the air. But still farther east, in the southeastern United States, you can find another wet region. Here warm, moist air blows inland from the Atlantic Ocean and the Gulf of Mexico. This air brings plenty of rain to the southeastern states. The northern states east of the Mississippi also receive ample moisture.

PEOPLE OF NORTH AMERICA

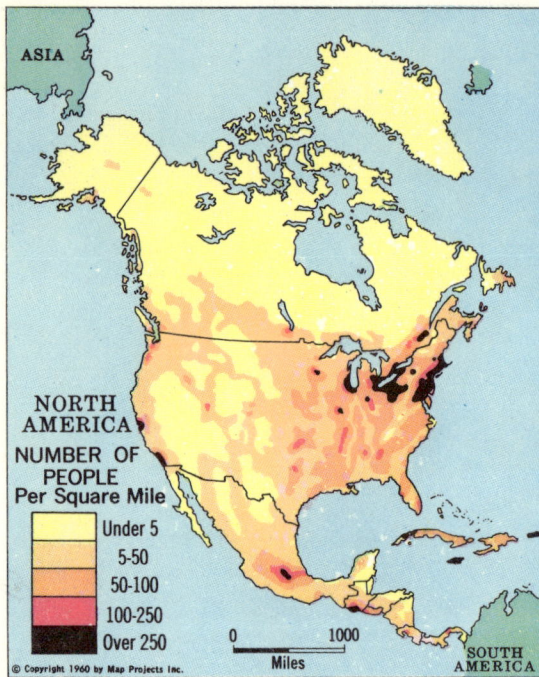

NORTH AMERICA
NUMBER OF PEOPLE
Per Square Mile

Under 5
5-50
50-100
100-250
Over 250

ASIA

SOUTH AMERICA

0   1000
Miles

© Copyright 1960 by Map Projects Inc.

These are the people of North America. Two hundred and fifty million strong, they have spread themselves across the continent. Eskimo, Indian, cowboy, statesman, factory worker, great planter, small farmer, doctor, fisherman, teacher, shopkeeper, miner, and sailor—all have found homes in North America.

People have been coming to this continent for thousands of years. A few came before the beginning of written history, but most have come in the last 400 years. And some are stepping off boats and airplanes this very day to begin a new life in the New World.

The first white men to make their homes in North America came from Spain. At the time they crossed the Atlantic Ocean from Europe, about five million Indians occupied North America.

Manhattan Island, in New York City, is North America's most densely populated area. People from every part of the world have come here to live. Four and a half million are of foreign origin.

Van Bucher—Photo Researchers

Royal Lowy—American Indian Archives

These Sioux Indians represent the 350,000 Indians that live in the United States today. Many more Indians live in Canada, Mexico, Central America, and the Caribbean, as well as in South America.

The great majority of the Indians lived in the more fertile regions of present-day Mexico and Central America. In fact, little more than one million of North America's Indians lived on the land that became Canada and the United States.

Spanish explorers tramped over a vast portion of North America. But in much of the land they explored, the Spaniards failed to find the treasures of gold and silver they were seeking. They soon turned their attention to Mexico, Central America, and the Caribbean islands.

Meanwhile, settlers from northwestern Europe began moving to North America. They built their homes in the portions of North America now occupied by Canada and the United States.

Frenchmen were Canada's first settlers. French settlers occupied the St. Lawrence Valley. They also built outposts on the Great Lakes. Eventually they claimed all the land drained by the Mississippi River.

Settlers from England arrived in North America after the French began their occupation of Canada. At first the English settled only on the east coast. People from Finland, Sweden, and the Netherlands also built settlements on the east coast.

Each country paid little attention to the claims of the others.

For many years European countries struggled to gain possession of North America. Englishmen took over the Finnish, Swedish, and Dutch settlements. England fought with France and Spain.

Less than one seventh of the people of the United States live on farms. USDA

Fred and Sara Machetanz

Eskimos are North America's northernmost people. They live by fishing and hunting.

Fritz Henle—Photo Researchers

Over nine tenths of Haiti's people are Negroes. The official language of Haiti is French.

When the United States freed itself from England, the struggle for control of the continent continued. Fortunately, much land changed hands by treaty or by purchase rather than by war. The United States thus obtained a vast area west of the Mississippi River from France in 1803,

Over 650 people per square mile crowd Puerto Rico. Yet more than half of the people are farmers.

Courtesy of the Puerto Rico News Service

Florida from Spain in 1819, and Alaska from Russia in 1867,

In the Caribbean islands, and in the land that was to become the southern states of the United States, large areas had to be cleared for farms. Few workers were available. At first the white men tried to force Indians to clear the forests and cultivate the crops. But Indians proved to be poor plantation workers.

To solve this labor problem, great numbers of Negroes were brought to North America from Africa. Today Negroes make up a large share of the population of many Caribbean islands. In the United States about one tenth of the population is Negro. In Central America many Negroes occupy coastal areas where they work on banana plantations. But in Mexico and Canada the number of Negroes is quite small.

Who are the people of North America? No place on earth has a more varied population. North America's people have come from every continent on earth except Antarctica, which had no people to send. Thousands crossed the ocean from all of the countries of Europe. Africa sent the ancestors of North America's Negroes. And Asia, too, sent its people to make new homes on the North American continent.

The people of North America are spread unevenly over the continent. Some parts of North America are almost empty of people. Other parts are only thinly settled—tiny communities are separated by miles and miles of empty land. And still other places in North America seem jammed with people.

Why are some places crowded and other places empty? For the most part, the people of North America have concentrated in those places best suited to support human life. They have gathered where the climate is desirable, or where the soil is most fertile, or where the mineral resources are richest.

You are probably interested in rockets and space travel. Many people are. But all of us need to remember that man has been earthbound for thousands of years. And we need to remember, too, that man still gets all of his food, his clothing, and his

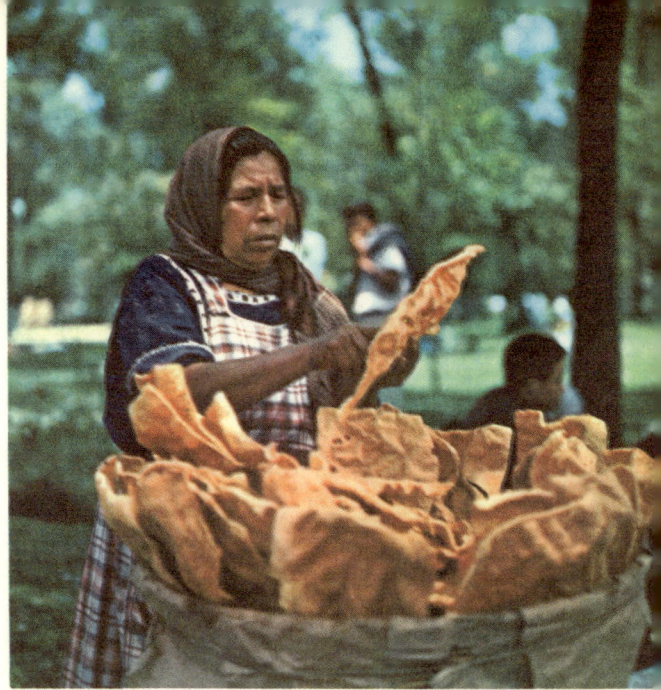

Jane Latta

Four fifths of Mexico's people are at least part Indian. Over one fourth are pure Indian.

shelter from the earth. To get these things man has sought out those places best suited to provide them. This book will help you see the kinds of places man has selected in North America.

Guatemala has Central America's largest population. Many are descendants of the ancient Mayans.

Courtesy of the Pan American Coffee Bureau

NORTH AMERICA

U.S.S.R.

ARCTIC OCEAN

BERING SEA

Wrangel I.

Bering Strait

BEAUFORT SEA

ALASKA

Arctic Circle

Bristol Bay

Kodiak I.

Alexander Archipelago

Queen Charlotte Islands

Vancouver Island

YUKON

BRITISH COLUMBIA

ALBERTA

Prince Patrick I.

Sverdrup Is.

Melville I.

Banks I.

Victoria Island

Prince of Wales I.

Ellesmere I.

Devon I.

BAFFIN BAY

Baffin Island

DAVIS STRAIT

GREENLAND (Denmark)

Denmark Strait

ICELAND

NORTHWEST TERRITORIES

Great Bear Lake

Great Slave Lake

Foxe Basin

Hudson Strait

C A N A D A

SASKATCHEWAN

MANITOBA

Lake Winnipeg

ONTARIO

HUDSON BAY

James Bay

QUEBEC

LABRADOR

NEWFOUNDLAND

NEWFOUNDLAND

Prince Edward Island

C. Breton I.

NEW BRUNS.

NOVA SCOTIA

PACIFIC OCEAN

WASHINGTON

OREGON

IDAHO

MONTANA

WYOMING

NORTH DAKOTA

SOUTH DAKOTA

MINNESOTA

L. Superior

WISC.

L. Michigan

MICHIGAN

L. Huron

MAINE

VT.

N.H.

NEW YORK

MASS.

CT.

R.I.

NEVADA

UTAH

CALIFORNIA

ARIZONA

COLORADO

NEBRASKA

KANSAS

IOWA

MISSOURI

ILLINOIS

IND.

OHIO

PENNA.

N.J.

MD.

DEL.

W. VA.

VIRGINIA

UNITED STATES

NEW MEXICO

OKLAHOMA

ARK.

KENTUCKY

TENNESSEE

NORTH CAROLINA

SOUTH CAROLINA

GEORGIA

MISS.

ALABAMA

TEXAS

LOUISIANA

FLORIDA

ATLANTIC OCEAN

NORTH AMERICA

Tropic of Cancer

Gulf of California

MEXICO

Gulf of Campeche

GULF OF MEXICO

Straits of Florida

Yucatán Channel

CUBA

Bahama Islands (Br.)

PUERTO RICO (U.S.A.)

HAITI

DOMINICAN REPUBLIC

Jamaica (W.I.)

CARIBBEAN SEA

BRITISH HONDURAS

GUATEMALA

EL SALVADOR

HONDURAS

NICARAGUA

COSTA RICA

PANAMA

Canal Zone (U.S.A.)

VENEZUELA

COLOMBIA

HAWAII

Kauai

Niihau

Oahu

Molokai

Lanai

Maui

Kahoolawe

Hawaii

PACIFIC OCEAN

0   50   100

Miles

160°   158°   156°

0   500   1000

Miles

© Copyright 1960 by Map Projects Inc.

TRANSPORTATION

The three maps on this page tell today's story of transportation in North America. In the thickly settled areas of the eastern United States and southern Canada, there is a dense network of highways, railroads, and air routes. Wherever there are many people and cities, an efficient transportation system is needed to keep them supplied with goods and carry them to their work. Transportation will only pay for itself if there are plenty of passengers and freight to be carried.

In the relatively empty spaces of northern Canada, the western United States, and Mexico and Central America, the population is sparse and the land is rugged. Because the population is small, there is not much traffic in passengers or freight. The rugged terrain makes construction expensive. In these regions it is neither necessary nor profitable to build a dense network of railroads and highways.

There are four million miles of highways in North America and 70 million motor vehicles. In the United States alone, freight trains carry over 40 million carloads of freight each year. And scheduled airlines fly nearly 800 million miles and carry 45 million passengers, not counting international operations.

NORTH AMERICA
MAIN AIR ROUTES

0 ——— 1000
Miles

© Copyright 1960 by Map Projects Inc.

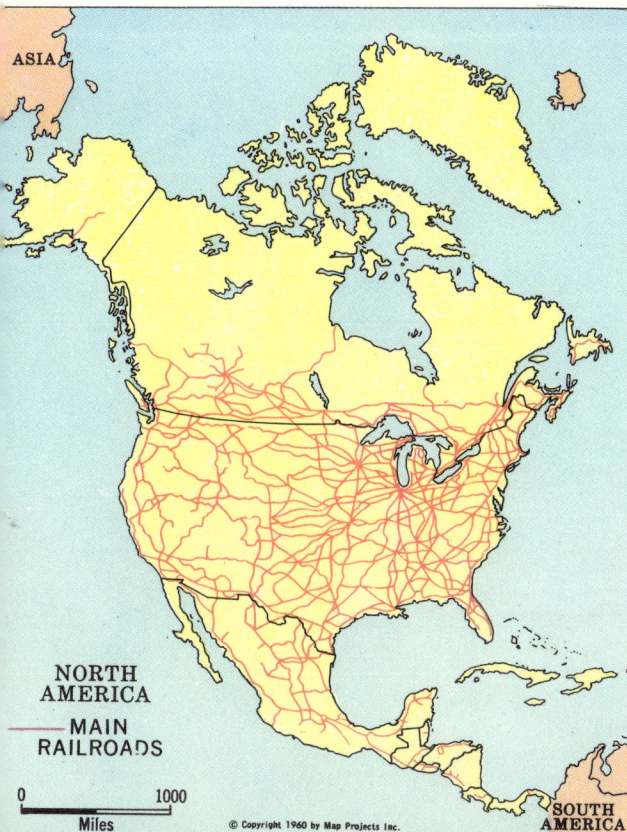

NORTH AMERICA
MAIN RAILROADS

0 ——— 1000
Miles

© Copyright 1960 by Map Projects Inc.

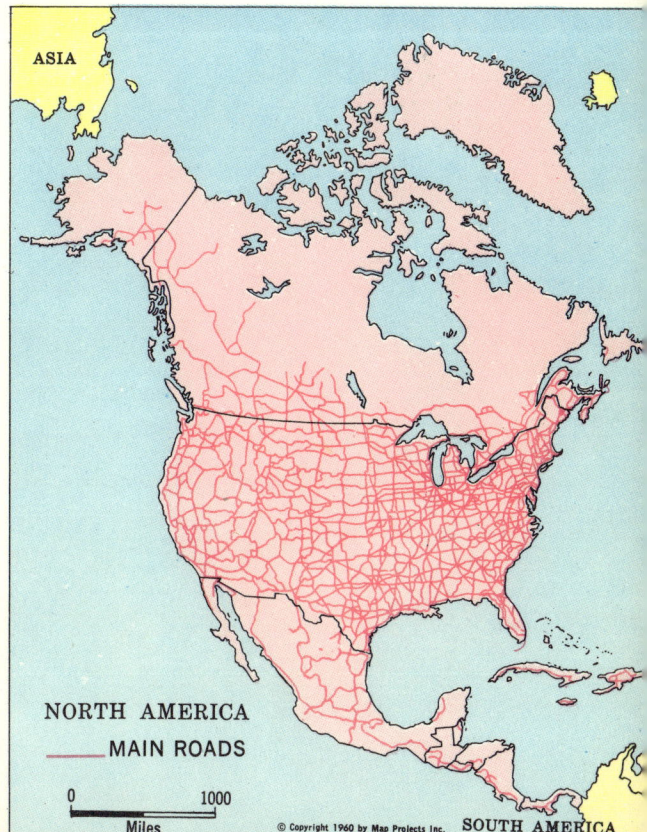

NORTH AMERICA
MAIN ROADS

0 ——— 1000
Miles

© Copyright 1960 by Map Projects Inc.

Ewing Galloway

Across the Hudson River are the famous skyscrapers of Manhattan Island, the center of New York. In 1626 the island was purchased from the Indians for $24 worth of trinkets by the West India Company. North America's largest city, New York is visited by millions of tourists each year.

Four million people in the Los Angeles metropolitan area make good use of their highways. This is one of North America's fastest-growing cities.

Ewing Galloway

Houston, Texas, is the South's largest city and the world's largest inland cotton market. Its port is connected by canal to the Gulf of Mexico.

Fred Bond—FPG

LEADING CITIES OF NORTH AMERICA

North America has some of the world's great cities. We are using the word "great" to mean cities with populations of over one million.

Eighteen of the world's 86 cities with more than one million people are in North America. Pictures of some of North America's great cities are on the following pages.

The world has had a few great cities for many years, but the growth of so many great cities is quite recent. It was not possible to feed the large number of people who now live in big cities until transportation facilities had been developed to bring food to them. The kind of transportation network that you see on page 15 has come about only in very recent times.

In the Old World, cities grew slowly over a long period of time. In North America, they grew rapidly. In many cases they started as wilderness communities. Most have grown to great cities in less than 100 years.

Courtesy of TWA—Trans World Airlines

The capital of the United States is Washington, D. C., a city site chosen by George Washington.

New York, North America's largest city, reached a population of one million in 1870. It was the first city in North America to have a population of one million. Today New York, its suburbs, and the nearby cities, have a total population of over 14 million. Nearly one person in every 18 in all of North America lives in the New York metropolitan area.

Across the historic Common is the city of Boston, site of many Revolutionary War landmarks.

Ewing Galloway

Philadelphia is a city rich in history. Its Independence Hall, where the Declaration of Independence was signed, houses the Liberty Bell.

Chicago, industrial and transportation center of the Midwest, is located on Lake Michigan. It is also famed for its meat packing industry.

Great cities do not grow large without reason. First, of course, many towns and cities had their beginnings as marketing and service centers for the surrounding agricultural region. But there are good geographic reasons for the location of large cities.

Many large cities came into being where natural routes of travel converge, or meet. Before the time of railroads and automobiles, large cities almost always were located on navigable water. Navigable water is water deep enough for large boats. Places along navigable rivers, oceans, and large lakes were good sites for cities.

One part of North America, called the American Manufacturing Belt, helps explain the growth of cities on this continent.

The American Manufacturing Belt is the great industrial workshop of the United States and Canada. It is mainly located in the northeastern United States, but it extends westward to include the southern Great Lakes. It also includes parts of Ontario and Quebec in Canada, and extends as far south as St. Louis and the Ohio River Valley.

The Golden Gate Bridge spans San Francisco Bay. San Francisco has a fine natural harbor.

Detroit, Michigan, is a great industrial city famous for its output of automobiles.

Cleveland, Ohio, on the shores of Lake Erie, is one of the Midwest's important manufacturing centers.

Most of North America's manufacturing is concentrated in or near big cities. More than 400 cities important for their manufacturing are located in the American Manufacturing Belt. Fifty of these cities are along the shores of the Atlantic Ocean and the southern Great Lakes. Well over 200 of the cities are on navigable rivers. Thirty are on canals that either were or are now important. Altogether over three out of every four cities in this region are on navigable water. Only 70 cities in the American Manufacturing Belt have no such location, and nearly all of these 70 cities owe their growth to important sites on railroad lines. It is easy to see how very important transportation has been to the growth of North American cities.

St. Louis stands just below the meeting place of the great Missouri and Mississippi Rivers.

Toronto's harbor and docking facilities on Lake Ontario help make it a manufacturing center.

In Montreal, Canada's largest city, both the French and English languages are used.

Havana is Cuba's capital and the largest city in the Caribbean. The Spanish-Colonial city attracts many tourists, especially in winter, because of its fine climate, its ocean beaches, and its gaiety.

Probably the oldest North American city, Mexico City is the capital of Mexico and one of the world's largest cities. Its wide avenues pass Aztec ruins, old Spanish churches, and ultra-modern buildings.

G. H. Jarrett—FPG

This bridge over the St. Lawrence Seaway connects two friendly neighbors—Canada and the United States.

CANADA,

LAND OF THE NORTH

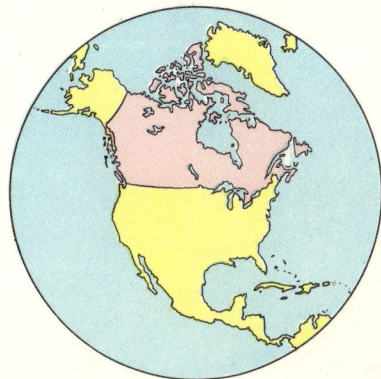

Canada is larger than the United States. It is even larger than all of Europe without the Soviet Union. Only two countries in all the world, the Soviet Union and China, have more territory than Canada.

Canada has nearly half the land of North America. Yet it has only one fifteenth of North America's people. Much of Canada is sparsely settled.

Unlike most countries, Canada has oceans on three of its borders. The Atlantic Ocean is on the east, the Pacific is on the west, and the Arctic Ocean is on the north. Canada's southern border meets the northern border of the United States. This is a friendly border. No forts are needed. The people of Canada and the United States like and respect each other.

Tiny fishing villages, like this one in Newfoundland, dot the shores of Canada's Atlantic Provinces. Their fishing fleets bring into port thousands of tons of fish each year.

Salmon have made the North Pacific coast one of North America's most important fishing regions.

Wealth from the Seas

Fishing was one of Canada's first industries. Fishermen from Europe are believed to have pulled great catches of fish from the waters off Newfoundland even before the first European explorers sighted the mainland of North America. These men, after crossing the Atlantic, would have fished a stormy, foggy area of shallow water called the Grand Banks.

The Grand Banks are still important as a source of fish. From southwestern New Brunswick to Labrador is a fishing coast 5,000 miles in length. This long shoreline, with its many good harbors and the abundant fish food found in the cool waters, make the ocean off eastern Canada one of the world's finest fishing grounds. Here are great schools of cod, herring, halibut, mackerel, and haddock.

Nearly every village along the coast of Nova Scotia, Newfoundland, and New Brunswick has its fleet of fishing vessels.

The poor soil and the cool climate of this region discourage farming. So for years men have turned to the sea to earn their living.

The fish resources of these waters are plentiful. In a recent year fishermen from the Atlantic Provinces of Canada caught more than 70 million dollars worth of fish.

Canada's Pacific coast is also famous for its fisheries. Deep fjords and a shallow ledge 50 to 100 miles offshore are fine feeding grounds for fish. Today British Columbia ranks close to the Atlantic Provinces in the value of its fish catch.

Salmon is "king" among fish on the Pacific coast. The sockeye salmon is especially important. Although other kinds of salmon grow larger than the 3- to 10-pound sockeye, none are more valued by the canning industry.

When the British Columbia salmon fleet comes into port, the fish are unloaded mechanically. Streams of fresh water wash them. Then the salmon are sent to the "dressing room." There a large machine cuts off heads, tails, fins, and scales. Next the salmon are thoroughly cleaned, sliced to proper size, put into cans, and cooked. And, finally, off the end of the "assembly line," comes a freshly labeled can of salmon ready for the grocer's shelf, where it is bought and taken home for a meal.

Cod drying in the sun is still a common sight in the Atlantic Provinces of Canada. But today great quantities of fish are quick-frozen or canned and shipped to all parts of the world.

E. B. Norwood—FPG

CANADA

Map labels and place names:

ARCTIC OCEAN
ALASKA (U.S.A.)
PARRY ISLANDS
Melville I.
Bathurst I.
Cornwallis I.
Ellesm...
De...
Banks I.
Prince Albert Peninsula
McClure Strait
Viscount Melville Sound
Lanc...
Prince of Wales I.
Somerset I.
Fort Ross
BEAUFORT SEA
Amundsen Gulf
Fort Collinson
DISTRICT VICTORIA ISLAND
Boothia Peninsula
Port Brabant
Aklavik
Fort McPherson
Arctic Red River
Harton R.
Wollaston Peninsula
Coppermine
Cambridge Bay
King William I.
McClintock Channel
Arctic Circle
Yukon R.
Porcupine R.
Dawson
Klondike
Mayo Landing
Snag
Aishihik
Ross River
Haines Junction
Whitehorse
YUKON
MACKENZIE MTS.
Fort Good Hope
Great Bear Lake
Norman Wells
Mackenzie R.
Sawmill Bay
NORTHWEST TER...
Perry River
Mt. Lucania 17,150'
Mt. Logan 19,850'
Gulf of Alaska
DISTRICT OF MACKENZIE
Contwoyto Lake
Back R.
DISTRICT OF KE...
Wrigley
MacKay Lake
Baker Lake
Mt. Hunt 9,000'
STIKINE MTS.
Teslin
Watson Lake
Teslin L.
Fort Simpson
Rae
Yellowknife
Fort Reliance
Chesterfield Inlet
Thelon R.
Kazan R.
Dease Lake
Fort Liard
Fort Providence
Great Slave L.
Tavani
Dubawnt Lake
Telegraph Creek
Hay River
Fort Resolution
Padlei
Maguse River
Nelson Forks
Fort Smith
Slave R.
Nueltin L.
Eskimo Point
COAST
Fort Nelson
CARIBOU MTS.
Fort Fitzgerald
Uranium City
Fond du Lac
Stony Rapids
ROCKY
Fort Grahame
Hazelton
Beatton River
Keg River
Peace R.
Fort Vermilion
Carcajou
L. Claire
BIRCH MTS.
L. Athabasca
Wollaston L.
Seal R.
Churchill R.
Prince Rupert
Skeena R.
Finlay Forks
BRITISH
Fort St. John
Hines Creek
Cree L.
Churchill
Cape Chur...
ALEXANDER ARCHIPELAGO
Massett
Smithers
Fort Fraser
Dawson Creek
Peace River
McLennan
Grande Prairie
Fort McMurray
Athabasca R.
Frobisher L.
Churchill L.
Peter Pond L.
Brochet
Egenolf L.
Reindeer Lake
Port Nelson
Sandspit
QUEEN CHARLOTTE ISLANDS
Hecate Strait
Ocean Falls
COLUMBIA
Prince George
Quesnel
CARIBOU MTS.
ALBERTA
White Court
Athabasca
Beauval
LaRonge
Meadow Lake
Sherridon
York F...
S. Indian Lake
Thicket Portage
Split L.
Ilford
Gillam
Amery
RANGE
Williams Lake
Dog Creek
Jasper
Barrhead
Bonnyville
St. Paul
Big River
Flin Flon
Cormorant
Wabowden
Norway House
Port Hardy
Mt. Waddington 13,260'
Edmonton
Vegreville
Camrose
North Battleford
Prince Albert
SASKATCHEWAN
MANITOBA
The Pas
MTS.
Lacombe
Red Deer
Penhold
Saskatchewan R.
LaRonge
Melfort
Nipawin
Tisdale
L. Winnipeg
Berens River
VANCOUVER ISLAND
Courtenay
Powell River
Kamloops
SELKIRK MTS.
Olds
Banff
Stettler
Hanna
Drumheller
Unity
Biggar
Rosthern
Humboldt
Saskatoon
Dafoe
Wynyard
Canora
Yorkton
Melville
Russell
Swan River
Winnipegosis
L. Winnipegosis
Sandy L.
Port Alberni
Nanaimo
New Westminster
Victoria
Vancouver
Penticton
Princeton
Kimberley
Coleman
Calgary
High River
Claresholm
Taber
Lethbridge
Cardston
Medicine Hat
Leader
Swift Current
Herbert
Moose Jaw
Watrous
Foam Lake
Broadview
Moosomin
Lake Manitoba
Cat La...
Red Lake
Gimli
Riverton
Lac Seul
Fraser R.
Castlegar
Cranbrook
Shaunavon
Assiniboia
Qu'Appelle
Regina
Weyburn
Carlyle
Rivers
Neepawa
Broadview
Selkirk
Winnipeg
Carman
Morden
Steinbach
Souris
Sioux L...
Kenora
Igna...
Rainy River
Fort Frances
Columbia R.
Estevan
Lake of the Woods
UNITED STA...

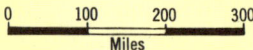

Craig Harbour

Dundas Harbour

BAFFIN BAY

Bay   Bylot
den   I.
en.   Pond
       Inlet

Clyde

BAFFIN ISLAND

GREENLAND
(Denmark)

Penny Highland

DAVIS STRAIT

TORIES

Melville
Peninsula

Prince
Charles I.

Cumberland
Peninsula

Cumberland Sound

FOXE BASIN

IN

Foxe
Pen.

Frobisher Bay
Hall
Peninsula

Frobisher Bay

Southampton
I.

Foxe Channel

HUDSON STRAIT

Coats I.

Mansel I.

Wolstenholme

Sugluk   Wakeham Bay

Cape Hopes
Advance   Akpatok I.

TORNGAT MTS.

Hebron

N

NEWFOUNDLAND

HUDSON BAY

Payne Bay

Ungava
Bay

George River

Nutak

Povungnituk

Leaf R.

Fort Chimo

Nain

LABRADOR

Makkovik

Port Harrison

L. Minto

Koksoak R.

Fort McKenzie

George R.

Hopedale

Rigolet

Cartwright

Belcher
Islands

Clearwater L.

Schefferville

Michikamau
Lake

North West River

Mealy
Mts.

Hamilton R.

Port Hope
Simpson

Port Saunders

Goose Bay

Battle Harbour

Forteau Bay   St. Anthony

Strait of Belle Isle

Fort Severn

Great Whale River

Great Whale R.

Fort
George

Kanaaupscow

Kaniapiskau
Lake

Nitchequon

Blanc Sablon

Roddickton

Notre Dame Bay

Harrington Harbour

Daniels
Harbour

Springdale   Botwood   Wesleyville

Bonavista
Carbonear

NEWFOUNDLAND

Winisk

Lake River

James

Akimiski I.

Sakami
Lake

Natashquan

Deer Lake

Grand
Falls

Gander

St. John's

Avalon
Peninsula

Lake

Attawapiskat

Bay

Eastmain

Eastmain
R.

QUEBEC

Sept Îles

Mingan

Anticosti I.

Corner Brook

Stephenville

Buchans

Port Aux Basques

Hermitage

Grand Bank

Trepassey

Cape Race

Fort Albany

Ogoki

Fort Hope

TARIO

Moosonee

Albany R.

Rupert House

Nemiscau

Lake Mistassini

Mistassini Post

Clarke City

Port Menier

St. Lawrence R.

Miquelon
(Fr.)

St. Pierre

GRAND
BANKS

Armstrong Station

Nakina

Pagwa
River

Hearst

Kapuskasing

Waswanipi

Gouin Res.

Chibougamau

Baie Comeau

Forestville

Mont Joli

Gaspé Peninsula

Gaspé

Chandler

Gulf of
St. Lawrence

Cabot
Strait

Sable I.

Geraldton

White
River

Oba

Cochrane

Smooth Rock Falls

St. Joseph d'Alma

Chicoutimi

Rimouski

Campbellton

Bathurst

PRINCE
EDWARD
ISLAND

Glace Bay

Inverness
Sidney

Cape Breton I.

pigon

Franz

Iroquois Falls

Timmins

Amos

Senneterre

Oskelaneo

Tadoussac

Riviere du Loup

Edmundston

Newcastle

Chatham

Charlottetown

New Glasgow

rt William

Michipicoten
Harbour

Foleyet

Kirkland Lake

Earlton

Noranda

Val d'Or

La Tuque

Quebec

Lévis

NEW
BRUNSWICK

Woodstock

Moncton

Amherst

New

Truro   Goldenville

ce

Superior

Chapleau

Gogama

Cobalt

Angliers

Cabonga
Res.

Shawinigan Falls

Thetford
Mines

Fredericton

St. John

Kingston

Digby

Dartmouth

Capreol

Timiskaming
Station

Mont Laurier

Trois Rivières

Granby

Mégantic

St. Stephen

Bridgewater

NOVA
SCOTIA

Sault Ste. Marie

Blind
River

Sudbury

North Bay

Fort Coulonge

Pembroke

MONTREAL

Sherbrooke

St. Stephen

Halifax

Georgian Bay

Parry Sound

Huntsville

Renfrew

Hull

Valleyfield

Bay of Fundy

Yarmouth

Lake

Huron

Owen
Sound

Orillia

Lindsay

Ottawa

Kingston

S

Kincardine

Barrie

Oshawa   Belleville

L. Ontario

Toronto

Hamilton

Kitchener   Brantford

Sarnia

London

Windsor

Chatham

Lake Erie

Lake Michigan

ATLANTIC   OCEAN

70° 60° 75° 50° 40° 70° 30° 65° 60°
80° 70° 60°
55° 50° 45° 40°

Logs come tumbling down swift Canadian streams on their way to the sawmill. About 46 percent of the land is forested.

Forestry and Furs

Few countries of the world have as great forest wealth as Canada. Only Canada's agricultural products are more valuable than its forest products.

Sawmills buzz with activity. British Columbia ranks first among Canada's provinces in the production of sawmill products. Quebec and Ontario rank second and third. These three provinces produce four fifths of Canada's sawmill products.

Here are the log-sorting ponds and the great sawmills of Victoria, British Columbia. Wood is also used in the pulp and paper industries.

Malak—Alpha

G. H. Jarrett—FPG

For over three hundred years trappers have taken beaver pelts from Canadian forests. Fur trappers were among the early explorers of North America.

These silver foxes are being raised on a Prince Edward Island fur farm. Mink and other animals are also raised on fur farms in Canada.

The Pacific mountain area is a land of forests. This is a region of softwoods (trees which have needles instead of broad leaves). Here grows some of the finest timber in North America. The most important timber tree of the Pacific coast is the giant Douglas fir.

The climate of the Pacific coast of Canada is mild even though this region is far to the north. Warm, damp air, blowing off the Pacific Ocean, gives the area a long growing season. Plenty of rain falls. Mild temperatures and heavy rainfall are ideal for rapid tree growth.

Pulpwood is also an important Canadian forest product. Paper is made from wood pulp. Canada's first pulp mill was built less than 100 years ago, but the industry has grown rapidly. Today more than 100 pulp and paper mills are busy at work.

Pulp and paper production have become important in Canada for several reasons. First, of course, is the tremendous supply of pulpwood available from Canada's forests. Canada's great supply of water power, which keeps the mills running, is also important. Important, too, is a good market in which to sell the product.

The United States, just south of the Canadian border, is Canada's best customer. The United States buys nearly all of Canada's exports of pulpwood. And the United States also buys more than four fifths of Canada's newsprint (the kind of paper on which newspapers are printed).

Furs were one of Canada's earliest products. Trappers explored much of the Canadian wilderness. A few trappers still follow their traplines through the snow-blanketed forests of the north country. But today most of Canada's fur comes from fur farms. Fur farming, where fox, mink, chinchilla, and martin are raised in captivity, started on Prince Edward Island. It proved so profitable that it quickly spread to the other provinces. Nearly 30 million dollars' worth of furs comes out of Canada each year.

This mine at Beaverlodge, Saskatchewan, is producing Canada's exciting new mineral resource—uranium.

Canada's Mineral Riches

Trapping brought a handful of settlers to Canada's north country. But mineral resources brought settlers by the thousands. Minerals of great value and variety are scattered over Canada. Of all the minerals discovered, none has created as much excitement as gold. It has been found from Newfoundland off the east coast to the Yukon Territory in the far northwest.

Because gold is so valuable for its weight, this precious metal can be mined in out-of-the-way places. Wherever a rich strike was made, a new mining camp sprang up. Shacks and stores were hurriedly built in places where no man had ever lived before. Many early mining camps were so isolated that they could only be reached by boat or by long difficult hikes overland. When the gold was mined out,

The Yellowknife Mine, on Great Slave Lake, produces a large share of Canada's gold.

the camps were deserted. Where big strikes were made, modern towns gradually replaced the rough-and-tumble mining camps. Much the same thing happens when gold is discovered today.

Canada ranks second only to South Africa as a producer of gold. Most of Canada's gold is mined in an area that reaches from central Ontario eastward into Quebec. This area is sometimes called the "Valley of Gold." In spite of all the gold that has been mined, it is believed that the surface has barely been scratched. Great quantities of gold remain in Canada for lucky prospectors to discover.

Sometimes prospectors hunting for gold find other valuable mineral resources. And sometimes tremendous deposits of minerals are found quite by accident. One of the most important of the early mining areas was in the vicinity of Sudbury. There, in the 1880's, rocks were being blasted to build a railroad. The blasting uncovered huge deposits of copper and nickel. Today the Sudbury district is still a great mining center. Three fourths of the world's supply of nickel is mined there. Nickel is added to steel to make it strong and hard. There is enough nickel left in the ground around Sudbury to keep the world supplied for another 100 years.

Copper and platinum are mined along with nickel at Sudbury. For every pound of nickel obtained, there is an added yield of two pounds of copper. Half of the world's supply of platinum also comes from the Sudbury mines.

Our growing industries need an ever-increasing supply of minerals. The search for these minerals is going on this very minute in northern Canada. But no longer are lonely prospectors combing the wilderness on foot. Modern mineral explorers, called geologists, are doing their prospecting from the air. The airplane, more than anything else, has opened up northern Canada. Air transport can carry geologists to the most isolated places. And the airplane can keep them supplied during the long, bitterly cold northern winter.

Steep Rock Mine, northwest of Lake Superior, is one of Canada's richest sources of iron ore.

G. H. Jarrett—FPG

G. H. Jarrett—FPG

Petroleum has fast become the leading mineral resource of Canada.

Malak—Annan Photo Features

Geologists today are often searching for new minerals needed by industry rather than for gold. One ore they are seeking is pitchblende, the source of radium and uranium. Pitchblende was first discovered in Canada at the eastern end of Great Bear Lake. A mining town, Port Radium, was built. Port Radium is just 28 miles south of the Arctic Circle.

New discoveries of pitchblende have recently been made. One important new pitchblende mine is at Uranium City, on the shores of Lake Athabaska. Uranium City has grown from a wilderness to a town of several thousand people in a few short years.

Iron ore is one of our most important minerals. A huge deposit of iron ore is now being mined in Canada. This deposit is in the lonely Ungava area on the Quebec-Labrador border. Ungava is an Eskimo word for "far away."

How to get this "far away" iron ore to the steel mills was a real problem. So engineers built a railroad, 360 miles long, from the mine to Seven Islands on the Gulf of the St. Lawrence. There ore freight ships load the iron to take it to the waiting blast furnaces of Canada and the United States.

Canada has huge supplies of coal. But Canada's coal is located in the wrong places. The industries that need coal are in the Great Lakes-St. Lawrence lowland, but three fifths of Canada's coal comes from far to the west in Alberta and British Columbia. Most of the rest is mined in the Atlantic Provinces. So the industrial lowland imports much coal from the United States.

Canada is rich in oil and natural gas. Just a few years ago a gigantic field of oil was found near Edmonton, Alberta. Oil production has grown rapidly. It now ranks first in value among Canada's mineral resources.

Coal is an important source of power for Canada's rapidly growing industries.

Quebec Province—Photo Driscoll

Tidy French farms, like this one on the Isle of Orleans, dot the Quebec landscape.

Canada's Farmlands

Farming is important to Canadians. More people in Canada are employed in farming than in any other industry.

There are two especially important farm areas in Canada. One is the Great Lakes and St. Lawrence lowland. The other is on the prairies of Manitoba, Saskatchewan, and Alberta. Both of these areas are in southern Canada. Farther north the growing season is too short for successful farming. This means that only a very small part of Canada's total land area can be used to produce crops.

The land in the Great Lakes and St. Lawrence lowland is sometimes called Canada's "Heartland." The "Heartland" is less than one tenth of Canada's total land area. Yet more than two thirds of the Canadian people live there. Four fifths of Canada's manufacturing is done in the "Heartland."

And it is there that half of Canada's farm products are raised.

The "Heartland" is important farming country for several reasons. Much of the area is level and easily tilled. It also has warmer summers than any other part of this great northern country. And the newly completed St. Lawrence Seaway provides this region with an excellent water route to the Atlantic Ocean and European markets.

The lowland along the Great Lakes and St. Lawrence River is part of a farm belt that also includes the northeastern United States. This farm belt is known as the hay and dairy region. Much of the land in Canada's hay and dairy region is stony. But such land often provides good pastures for dairy cattle. The summer weather is ideal for growing hay and oats. These crops make good feed for dairy cattle during the winter months when they must be fed in barns.

Tom Hollyman—Photo Researchers

A farmer in Alberta harvests wheat, the leading crop of Alberta, Saskatchewan, and Manitoba.

From the Gulf of Mexico to the Arctic Ocean is a broad area of plains. The Canadian portion of these plains is a grassland. Manitoba, Saskatchewan, and Alberta occupy this grassland. Together they are known as the Prairie Provinces.

The Prairie Provinces have been farming country ever since the first settlers arrived. The soil is rich, but the growing season is short, and there is often a shortage of rain. The choice of crops that can be grown under these conditions is very limited.

Wheat is king in the Prairie Provinces. More than three-fourths of the cropland is in wheat. Farmers grow as much wheat as possible. Wheat can get along with little rainfall. It will ripen quickly. And Europe provides a good market for Canadian wheat.

The rich soil of the Prairie Provinces has made this region the "breadbasket" of Canada.

G. H. Jarrett—FPG

George Hunter—Shostal

This farm, on the Peace River, belongs to a modern pioneer who is working land never before cultivated.

In the drier portions of the Prairie Provinces are Canada's ranches. These ranches are huge. Ranches often have thousands of head of cattle in a single herd. A hundred farms from the "Heartland" could be placed on one prairie cattle ranch.

Some parts of Canada grow special crops. The Annapolis-Cornwallis Valley in Nova Scotia is known the world over for its fine apples. Harvests of delicious grapes and peaches come from the Niagara Peninsula in Ontario. Northwestern New Brunswick and Prince Edward Island grow huge potato crops.

Only a tiny portion of rugged, forested British Columbia is suited for farming. Even so, British Columbia's farmers have their special crops—berries, fruit, vegetables, and flowering bulbs. Dairying is also important near the larger towns.

These Hereford cattle are part of a vast herd on a ranch in Alberta.

Most of British Columbia's farms are concentrated near the mouth of the Fraser River and in the southern portion of Vancouver Island. These locations get abundant rainfall, and their long growing season is another advantage.

Clemson—Annan Photo Features

Courtesy of Aluminium Limited, Montreal

A section of the smelter at the Kitimat plant of the Aluminum Company of Canada, the largest in the world

Canada's Growing Industry

Canada is rapidly becoming one of the world's leading manufacturing nations. The center of this manufacturing is the Great Lakes and St. Lawrence lowland. Here is where the raw materials from the rest of Canada flow in to be converted into manufactured goods.

Mineral ore, pulpwood, and timber move southward toward this "Heartland" from the mines and forests of Ontario and Quebec. From the Prairie Provinces come wheat, meat, and oil. And from the Atlantic Provinces come coal, wood, and food products.

Much of the power that turns the wheels of Canada's industry comes from the

Processing butter in a dairy-products plant

Malak—Annan Photo Features

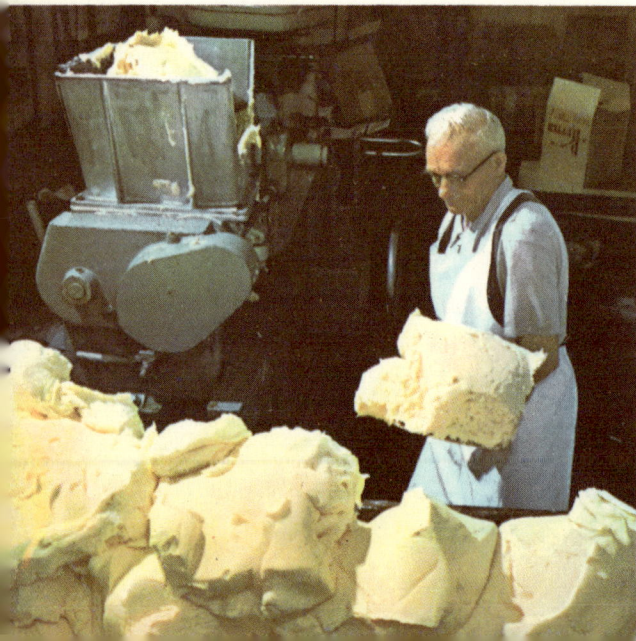

The paper industry depends on timber resources.

Malak—Annan Photo Features

streams that tumble down onto the lowland. Niagara Falls also provides great quantities of power. This waterpower is used to generate electricity. Canadian industry uses tremendous quantities of electricity.

Canada's industrial lowland extends from Windsor, just across the border from Detroit, through Toronto, Montreal, and on to Quebec. Throughout this region a dense network of railroads and highways provides needed land transportation. In addition, the great new St. Lawrence Seaway provides the cheap water transportation so necessary for shipping heavy or bulky goods.

What are Canada's chief manufactures? Pulp and paper rank first. Few places in the world are better located for the manufacture of pulp and paper than the St. Lawrence River Valley. Forests lie to the north. Markets in the United States are to the south. And the water power so important to this industry is available in abundance.

Water power also helps other Canadian industries. It is used by the rapidly-growing aluminum industry in both the St. Lawrence River valley and in British Columbia. The manufacture of newsprint, plastics, textiles, and chemicals all require

Malak—Annan Photo Features

In this plant at Sarnia, Ontario, synthetic rubber is manufactured from available raw materials.

great quantities of water and electricity.

Iron and steel manufacturing has long been a leading Canadian industry. Hamilton, Ontario, is sometimes called the "Pittsburgh of Canada."

Canada is one of the world's great trading nations. Canada buys and sells on a world market. Before World War II, the United Kingdom was Canada's best customer. But today, Canada's neighbor to the south, the United States, is its number one customer.

The Dominion Foundry and Steel plant at Hamilton, Ontario, one of Canada's large steel mills

G. H. Jarrett—FPG

CANADA

WASHINGTON

Port Angeles
Bellingham
Bremerton
Everett
Tacoma
Seattle
Aberdeen
Olympia
Mt. Rainier – 14,408'
Chehalis
Colville
Spokane
Newport
Sandpoint
Astoria
St. Helens
Longview
Vancouver
Yakima
Richland
Walla Walla
Pendleton
Ellensburg
Moscow
Lewiston
Kalispell
Havre
Great Falls
Missoula
Helena
Anaconda
Butte
Bozeman
Livingston
Dillon
Salmon
Roundup
Billings
Hardin
Miles City
Glendive

Portland
Mt. Hood – 11,245'
Salem
Corvallis
Albany
Eugene
Springfield
Coos Bay
Roseburg
Bend
Burns
Grants Pass
Medford
Crescent City
Klamath Falls
Steens Mts.

CASCADE RANGE
BLUE MTS.
La Grande
Baker

OREGON

HARNEY BASIN

Grangeville

BITTERROOT RANGE

ROCKY

MONTANA

Williston
Minot
Rugby
Devils Lake
Dickinson
Mandan
Bismarck
Jamesto

NORTH DAKOTA

Caldwell
Boise
Jerome
Twin Falls
Idaho Falls
Pocatello

IDAHO
Borah Peak 12,655'

Cody
Sheridan

WYOMING

Jackson
Thermopolis
Gannett Peak 13,785'
Lander
Green River
Rock Springs
Rawlins
Laramie
Cheyenne

Yellowstone Lake

MOUNTAINS

Lemmon
Mobridge
Eureka
Aberdeen
Belle Fourche
Sturgis
Lead
Pierre
Huron
Hot Springs
Midland
Belvedere
White River
Mitchel
Yan

SOUTH DAKOTA
BLACK HILLS

Marsland
Valentine
O'Neill
Ewing
Alliance
Scottsbluff
Sidney
Ogallala
North Platte
Kearney
Grand Island
Holdrege
Hasting
McCook
Norton

NEBRASKA

Mt. Shasta 14,162'
Eureka
Cape Mendocino
Lassen Peak 10,453'
Black Rock Desert
Winnemucca
Elko

COAST RANGES
GREAT
NEVADA
BASIN

Colusa
Santa Rosa
Berkeley
San Francisco
Oakland
San Jose
Monterey
Sacramento
Stockton
Reno
Sparks
Carson City
Austin
Eureka
Ely
L. Tahoe

CALIFORNIA
SIERRA NEVADA
COAST RANGES

Merced
Fresno
Mt. Whitney 14,496'
Bakersfield
Santa Maria
Santa Barbara
Pasadena
LOS ANGELES
Long Beach
Santa Ana
San Bernardino
San Diego
Brawley
El Centro

UTAH
Logan
Ogden
Salt Lake City
Tooele
Provo
Springville
Price
Nephi
Richfield
Cedar City

Great Salt Lake
Sevier L.

Craig
Grand Junction
Delta
Montrose
Durango
Alamosa

COLORADO
Denver
Aurora
Englewood
Boulder
Ft. Collins
Greeley
Sterling

Pikes Peak
Colorado Springs
Salida 14,110'
Pueblo
La Junta
Blanca Peak 14,363'

Platte

Goodland
Concordia
Hays
Great Bend
Garden City
Larned
Dodge City
Wich

KANSAS
Smoky Hill
Arkansas

Yucca Flats
North Las Vegas
Las Vegas
Boulder City
Death Valley

Grand Canyon

Kingman
Grand Canyon
Flagstaff
Gallup
Los Alamos
Sante Fe
Taos
N. Truchas Peaks 13,310'
Clayton
Raton

ARIZONA
Prescott
Baldy Peak 11,590'
Phoenix
Mesa
Miami
Globe
Morenci
Gila Bend
Eloy
Ajo
Tucson
Nogales
Douglas
Yuma

Salton Sea

NEW MEXICO
Farmington
Albuquerque
Tucumcari
Belen
Socorro
Clovis
Portales
Hereford
Childress
Roswell
Lovington
Silver City
Las Cruces
Alamogordo
Carlsbad
Hobbs
El Paso

Elephant Butte Res.

Dalhart
Borger
Pampa
Amarillo
Clinton
Woodward
Altus

OKLA
Oklahoma City
Ardm

Levelland
Lubbock
Wichita Falls
Lamesa
Graham
For Wor
Clebu
Odessa
Abilene
Breckenridge
Stephenville
San Angelo
Brady
Pecos
Fort Stockton
Alpine

EDWARDS PLATEAU

TEXAS

Del Rio
Uvalde
San Anto
Austin
Cor
Ch
Kingsvil
Laredo

Rio Grande

MEXICO

PACIFIC OCEAN

ALASKA inset

ARCTIC OCEAN
Pt. Barrow
Barrow
C. Lisburne
Chukchi Sea
U.S.S.R.
Noatak
Kotzebue
Selawik
Fort Yukon

BROOKS RANGE

Seward Pen.
Nome
Unalakleet

ALASKA
Holy Cross
Fairbanks
Mt. McKinley 20,320'
Palmer
Anchorage
Kenai
Valdez
Cordova
Skagway
Juneau
Douglas

Yukon
Tanana R.
Kuskokwim R.

CANADA

St. Lawrence I.
C. Romanzof
Nunivak I.
Bethel
Dillingham
Bristol Bay

BERING SEA

Alaska Peninsula
Chignik
Kodiak
Kodiak I.
Homer
Seldovia
Seward
Hoonah
Sitka
Petersburg
Wrangell
Ketchikan
Craig
Metlakatla

Gulf of Alaska

ALEXANDER ARCHIPELAGO

Unimak I.
Dutch Harbor

ALEUTIAN ISLANDS

PACIFIC OCEAN

Miles 0 300

HAWAII inset

Kauai
Kapaa
Lihue
Niihau

Kauai Channel

Oahu
Waialua
Wahiawa
Nanakuli
Lanikai
Waipahu
Honolulu

Kaiwi Channel

Molokai
Wailuku
Makawao
Lanai City
Lanai
Maui
Kahoolawe

Alenuihaha Channel

Hawi
Mauna Kea 13,796'
Mauna Loa 13,680'
Pahala
South Cape

PACIFIC OCEAN

Miles 0 50 100

C A N A D A

MINNESOTA
Lake of the Woods
International Falls
Red Lakes
Bemidji
Grand Rapids
Ely
Two Harbors
Hancock
Brainerd
Fergus Falls
Sauk Centre
Little Falls
St. Cloud
Crystal
St. Paul
Minneapolis
St. Peter
Pipestone
Red Wing
Mankato
Winona
Worthington
Austin

Lake Superior
Duluth
Superior
Ashland
Ironwood
Marquette
Munising
Iron Mountain
Saint Ignace
Spooner
Rhinelander
Antigo
Rice Lake
WISCONSIN
Stevens Point
Wisconsin Rapids
Green Bay
Oshkosh
Fond du Lac
Petoskey
Alpena
Traverse City
Manistee

MICHIGAN
L. Michigan
L. Huron
Saginaw
Flint
Pontiac
Grand Rapids
Lansing
Kalamazoo
Benton Harbor
Jackson
Dearborn
DETROIT
L. Erie
Erie

IOWA
Estherville
Algona
Fort Dodge
Sioux City
Perry
Ames
Maryville
Des Moines
Council Bluffs
Omaha
Indianola
Centerville
Oskaloosa
Cedar Rapids
Waterloo
Decorah
Davenport
Rock Island
Moline
Clinton

WISCONSIN Madison Milwaukee Racine Kenosha
Baraboo Watertown Janesville Platteville La Crosse

ILLINOIS
CHICAGO
Evanston
Aurora
Joliet
Kankakee
Rockford
Peoria
Bloomington
Springfield
Decatur
Quincy
Hannibal
Moberly
Kirksville
Litchfield
Granite City
East St. Louis
Centralia
Herrin
Marion
Cairo

INDIANA
Gary
South Bend
Fort Wayne
Muncie
Indianapolis
Terre Haute
Bloomington
Vincennes
New Albany
Evansville

OHIO
Toledo
Findlay
Lima
Piqua
Springfield
Dayton
Cincinnati
Columbus
Zanesville
Marietta
Covington
Ashland
Lorain
Akron
Canton
Warren
Youngstown
Cleveland

MISSOURI
Kansas City
Kansas City
Topeka
Fort Scott
St. Joseph
Excelsior Springs
Independence
Sedalia
Jefferson City
Lebanon
OZARK
Joplin
Neosho
Springfield
St. Louis
Cape Girardeau
Sikeston
Poplar Bluff
Caruthersville
Pocahontas
Jonesboro
Searcy

KANSAS
KENTUCKY
Paducah
Frankfort
Lexington
Louisville
Bowling Green
Hopkinsville
Somerset
Middlesboro
Hazard
Bristol

TENNESSEE
Nashville
Clarksville
Jackson
Memphis
West Memphis
Chattanooga
Knoxville
Oak Ridge
Johnson City
Cleveland

ARKANSAS
MTS.
Fayetteville
Batesville
Fort Smith
Little Rock
Hot Springs
Clarksdale
Bartlesville
Tulsa
Muskogee
McAlester
Antlers
Hugo
Paris
Texarkana
Marshall
Tyler
Palestine

MISS.
Tupelo
Aberdeen
Greenville
Yazoo City
Jackson
Vicksburg
Natchez
McComb
Picayune
Laurel
Hattiesburg
Meridian
Corinth
Gadsden

ALABAMA
Birmingham
Tuscaloosa
Selma
Montgomery
Phenix City
Eufaula
Dothan
Mobile
Pensacola

LOUISIANA
Shreveport
Mansfield
Ferriday
Alexandria
Lake Charles
New Iberia
Baton Rouge
Houma
New Orleans
Beaumont
Houston
Port Arthur
Galveston
Bay City
Bastrop
Monroe
Camden
El Dorado
Hope

GEORGIA
Rome
Marietta
Atlanta
Augusta
Macon
Columbus
La Grange
Dublin
Baxley
Dawson
Albany
Fitzgerald
Waycross
Valdosta
Brunswick
Savannah

SOUTH CAROLINA
Greenville
Anderson
Columbia
Rock Hill
Dillon
Florence
Orangeburg
Georgetown
Charleston
Beaufort

NORTH CAROLINA
Winston-Salem
High Point
Greensboro
Durham
Raleigh
Charlotte
Gastonia
Asheville
Salisbury
Fayetteville
Wilmington
Newport News
Elizabeth City

VIRGINIA
Richmond
Petersburg
Roanoke
Lynchburg
Danville
South Boston
Norfolk
Portsmouth
Henderson
Bluefield
Bristol

W. VA.
Charleston
Huntington
Parkersburg
Fairmont
Martinsburg

PENNSYLVANIA
Pittsburgh
Johnstown
Harrisburg
York
PHILADELPHIA
Scranton
Wilkes-Barre
Emporium
Erie
Paterson
Newark
NEW YORK
Trenton
Camden
Wilmington
Atlantic City
Dover
MD.
DEL.
Baltimore
Annapolis
Arlington
Alexandria
Fredericksburg
Salisbury
Washington, D.C.

NEW YORK
Buffalo
Niagara Falls
Rochester
Syracuse
Utica
Schenectady
Albany
Binghamton
Elmira
Poughkeepsie
Yonkers
Adirondack Mts.
Watertown
Ogdensburg
Plattsburgh
Burlington

MAINE
Fort Kent
Caribou
Millinocket
Bangor
Belfast
Augusta
Auburn
Bath
Portland

VT.
Montpelier
Rutland
Bennington

N.H.
Berlin
Laconia
Concord
Manchester
Portsmouth

MASS.
Worcester
Springfield
BOSTON
Providence
New Bedford
R.I.
Newport
CT.
Hartford
New Haven
Bridgeport
New London

L. Ontario
St. Lawrence R.
L. Champlain
Moosehead L.

ATLANTIC OCEAN
Cape Hatteras
Cape Canaveral
BAHAMA ISLANDS

FLORIDA
Jacksonville
St. Augustine
Ormond Beach
Daytona Beach
Ocala
Sanford
Orlando
Tampa
Lakeland
Vero Beach
Fort Pierce
Clearwater
St. Petersburg
Sarasota
Arcadia
West Palm Beach
Fort Myers
Lake Okeechobee
Fort Lauderdale
Hialeah
Miami
Coral Gables
Key West
Tallahassee
Live Oak
Panama City
Biloxi
Gulfport
Marianna

GULF OF MEXICO
Straits of Florida
Tropic of Cancer

APPALACHIAN MTS.
Ohio R.
Mississippi R.
Missouri R.
Arkansas R.
Tennessee R.

Legend

NEW YORK	Over 1,000,000 population
Toledo	250,000–1,000,000 population
Pasadena	100,000–250,000 population
Decatur	50,000–100,000 population
Temple	Under 50,000 population

© Copyright 1960 by Map Projects Inc.

UNITED STATES

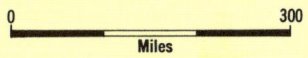

0 ——— 300
Miles

◉ National Capital
◎ State Capitals

USDA

Under the shadow of the majestic Rocky Mountains, a herd of fine beef cattle grazes in a high meadow in Wyoming. Note the winding pattern of the stream that carries away water from melting snow.

THIS IS THE U.S.A.

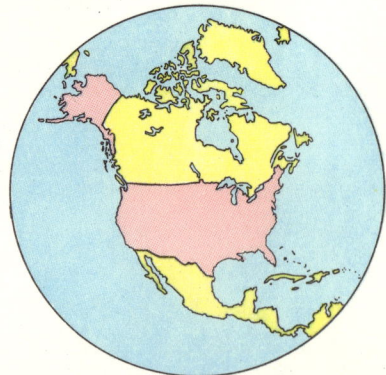

Ask someone to measure a mile for you. Then imagine a square, one mile on each side. Three and a half million of these squares could fit in the United States of America. And 180 million men, women, boys, and girls share this land.

Just 350 years ago the first settlers arrived from Europe. And less than 200 years ago the United States became a free and independent country. Since that time great progress has been made.

The first settlers landed on the East Coast. They began clearing the forests and plowing the soil. Settlers moved westward, ever seeking better land and greater opportunities. In this way the frontier moved

Cv La Tour—Photo Library

Half a million workers use 140 million tons of iron ore each year to produce steel.

across the United States, from the Atlantic to the Pacific.

It was slow work opening up the eastern third of the country. This eastern portion of the United States was covered with a great forest—one of the largest and densest in all the world. The land had to be cleared for cultivation. This hard work had to be done by hand. These early settlers had no bulldozers or tractors. They did not even have steel plows, but used plows that were made of wood.

The Appalachian Highlands also acted as a barrier to slow the westward movement of settlers. But once across the Highlands, a great fertile land of prairies and plains invited rapid settlement.

The large number of European immigrants who flocked to the United States furnished a steady stream of settlers to open these new lands. The government also helped by making free land available and by furnishing aid in building railroads, roads, and canals.

Farmers of the United States grow more food on less land than ever before. And it takes fewer farmers to grow this food. Better seed and fertilizer, mechanical equipment, and new methods of cultivating have all brought about these changes.

Rich deposits of iron ore and coal helped the United States develop a huge iron and steel industry. This iron and steel industry, in turn, formed the basis for much of the country's industrial development. A great variety of natural resources has made it possible for the United States to maintain ever-expanding industries.

Because of its climate, fertile soils, and variety of mineral and fuel resources, the people of the United States have long enjoyed great prosperity as compared with many of the countries of the world. The United States has only five per cent of the world's land area and less than seven per cent of the world's people. Yet the people of the United States consume nearly half of all that the world produces.

NORTHEASTERN UNITED STATES

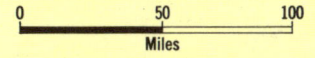

States: MAINE, VERMONT, NEW HAMPSHIRE, NEW YORK, MASSACHUSETTS, CONNECTICUT, RHODE ISLAND, NEW JERSEY, DELAWARE

Regions/Features: CANADA, ADIRONDACK MTS., CATSKILL MTS., GREEN MTS., WHITE MOUNTAINS, BLUE MTS., BERKSHIRE MTS., POCONO MTS., ATLANTIC OCEAN, Cape Cod, Long Island, Nantucket I., Martha's Vineyard, Block I., Montauk Point

Rivers/Lakes: St. Lawrence R., L. Champlain, L. George, Moosehead L., Chamberlain L., Chesuncook L., Flagstaff L., Sebago L., L. Winnipesaukee, Oneida L., St. John R., Aroostook R., Penobscot Bay, Delaware Bay, Long Island Sound, Cape Cod Bay, Chesapeake Bay

Peaks: Mt. Katahdin 5,268', Mt. Washington 6,288', Whiteface Mt. 4,867'

Cities (selected):
Madawaska, St. Agatha, Van Buren, St. Francis, Fort Kent, Allagash, Eagle Lake, Caribou, Fort Fairfield, Portage, Ashland, Presque Isle, Mars Hill, Clayton Lake, Masardis, Monticello, Houlton, Oakfield, Island Falls, Sherman Mills, Danforth, Millinocket, Jackman, Rockwood, Brownville, Springfield, Lincoln, Woodland, Calais, Eastport, Eustis, Dover-Foxcroft, Olamon, Wesley, Dennysville, Machias, Stratton, Rangeley, Bingham, Dexter, Milford, Bangor, Brewer, Orono, Old Town, Columbia Falls, Cherryfield, Jonesport, Anson, Skowhegan, Pittsfield, Fairfield, Bucksport, Mexico, Rumford, Farmington, Jay, Wilton, Waterville, Winslow, Searsport, Bar Harbor, Mt. Desert I., Bethel, Norway, Augusta, Winthrop, Hallowell, Gardiner, Belfast, Camden, Stonington, Swans I., Isle au Haut, Bridgton, Auburn, Lewiston, Lisbon, Wiscasset, Damariscotta, Rockland, Westbrook, Saco, Portland, South Portland, Old Orchard Beach, Biddeford, Kennebunk, Brunswick, Bath, Boothbay Harbor

Colebrook, Errol, Stratford, West Burke, Berlin, Newport, Orleans, Barton, Hardwick, Essex, St. Johnsbury, Lyndon, Swanton, St. Albans, Burlington, Montpelier, Bristol, Barre, Danville, Lisbon, Haverhill, Warren, Conway, Wolfeboro, Middlebury, Randolph, Bethel, Brandon, West Rutland, Proctor, Rutland, Hanover, Lebanon, Enfield, Laconia, Rochester, Berwick, Kittery, Portsmouth, Durham, Exeter, Derry, Poultney, Ludlow, Springfield, Manchester, Charlestown, Newport, Concord, Goffstown, Manchester, Jaffrey, Nashua, Bellows Falls, Newfane, Bennington, Brattleboro, Keene, Hinsdale, Winchendon, Haverhill, Lowell, Lawrence, Gloucester, Lynn, Somerville, Boston, Brookline, Quincy, Brockton, Provincetown, Barnstable, Hyannis

North Adams, Adams, Pittsfield, Greenfield, Gardner, Fitchburg, Cambridge, Athol, Great Barrington, Northampton, Holyoke, Worcester, Westfield, Springfield, Milford, Norwood, Taunton, Plymouth, Middleboro, Norfolk, Windsor, Manchester, Woonsocket, Pawtucket, Providence, Cranston, Fall River, New Bedford, Hartford, Waterbury, Meriden, Wallingford, Groton, Westerly, Hamden, New Haven, New London, Danbury, Bridgeport, Norwalk, Stamford, Greenport, Southampton, Montauk, Kings Park, Huntington, Patchogue, Sayville, Bay Shore, Lindenhurst, Glen Cove

Massena, Ogdensburg, Malone, Dannemora, Rouses Point, Chazy, Plattsburgh, Keeseville, Potsdam, St. Regis Falls, Gabriels, Saranac Lake, Lake Placid, Hammond, Gouverneur, Antwerp, Clayton, Harrisville, Carthage, Tupper Lake, Newcomb, Watertown, Big Moose, Blue Mountain Lake, Ticonderoga, Lowville, Old Forge, Speculator, Lake George, Glens Falls, Pulaski, Boonville, Remsen, Mexico, Camden, Fulton, Rome, Little Falls, Gloversville, Johnstown, Saratoga Springs, Amsterdam, Baldwinsville, Syracuse, Utica, Herkimer, Schenectady, Cohoes, Troy, Cazenovia, Hamilton, Watervliet, Albany, Rensselaer, Valatie, Cortland, Norwich, Oneonta, Milford, Cairo, Ravena, Greene, Sidney, Catskill, Hudson, Binghamton, Downsville, Phoenicia, Saugerties, Endicott, Deposit, Roscoe, Kingston, New Paltz, Susquehanna, Forest City, Liberty, Monticello, Newburgh, Beacon, Carbondale, Dickson City, Middletown, Poughkeepsie, Hyde Park, Scranton, Pittston, Port Jervis, West Point, Peekskill, Kingston, Wilkes-Barre, Freeland, Sussex, Ossining, Berwick, Stroudsburg, Newton, Sparta, Yonkers, Mt. Vernon, Shenandoah, Easton, Phillipsburg, Paterson, Passaic, Newark, New York, Jersey City, Bethlehem, Allentown, Clinton, Elizabeth, Perth Amboy, Bayonne, Emmaus, Reading, Lansdale, New Brunswick, Princeton, Red Bank, Pottstown, Norristown, Freehold, Asbury Park, Trenton, New Lakewood, Lancaster, Bristol, Philadelphia, Camden, Collingswood, Gloucester City, Barnegat, Coatesville, Chester, Wilmington, Pitman, Hammonton, Elkton, Newark, Salem, Vineland, Egg Harbor City, Pleasantville, Aberdeen, Bridgeton, Millville, Port Norris, Atlantic City, Ocean City, Chestertown, Dover, Frederica, Smyrna, Wildwood, Cape May, Lewes, Centreville, Denton, Easton, Harrington, Seaford, Laurel, Cambridge, Hebron, Princess Anne, Salisbury, Ocean City, Berlin, Snow Hill, Pocomoke City

Derby Line

THE NORTHEAST

It is hard to think of an industry that is not found in the northeastern states. Here is the greatest concentration of manufacturing in the United States. The factories of the Northeast turn out goods as varied as giant locomotives and delicate scientific instruments. Textiles ranging from the finest silk to the heaviest canvas are woven in northeastern mills. Paper and pens; airplanes and atomic submarines; shirts and shoes; guns and gasoline; chocolate and cement; rockets and radios; watches and woolens—all these products and many more are manufactured in the Northeast.

The Northeast is where American manufacturing began. The first factories were in New England. They produced cotton cloth. Why did this industry begin in New England? Here are some of the reasons:

Frank Donato—Photo Researchers

The Slater Textile Mill, in Pawtucket, R. I., was America's earliest factory.

Pittsburgh, at the junction of the Allegheny and Monongahela Rivers, is North America's steel center.

USDA

Forests of the Northeast and Canada provide the raw material for this paper mill in Maine.

1. New England had plenty of water-power to turn the mill wheels.
2. New England's damp air kept fibers from twisting and snarling during spinning.
3. There was a good supply of labor in this most densely settled part of the United States.
4. Because so many people lived in the Northeast, a good market was available.

The last two reasons have helped the Northeast keep its lead as the country's manufacturing center.

Power and raw materials are the basic ingredients of industry. Both are available in the northeastern states. Coal, natural gas, oil, and, of course, water power have long kept the Northeast well supplied with power.

A tremendous variety of raw materials is available—both hard and soft wood for furniture, paper, and pulp; fruits and vegetables for canning; fish for food and fertilizer; clay for pottery and bricks; shale and limestone for cement; and granite and marble for building stone.

But some of the Northeast's greatest industries depend on raw materials that must be imported. Almost all of the cotton, wool, silk, iron, copper, lead, zinc, rubber, and leather that flow into the Northeast's mills and factories are shipped into this region. This means that the Northeast has to have a good transportation system. Railroads, highways, and the sea lanes of the Atlantic Ocean all serve the industrial Northeast.

New York's crowded harbor serves the world's busiest port. It handles 400 ships a day.

Arthur Griffin—FPG

Two New England lobstermen unload their catch taken from the cold Atlantic Ocean waters.

Francis Pfotenhauer—Shostal

Northeastern Fisheries

Fishermen came first to North America. They charted the course across the North Atlantic Ocean that was followed by thousands of settlers. And fish was among the first resources of North America used by Europeans.

The first recorded fishing voyage off the coast of the northeastern United States was made in 1602, 18 years before the Pilgrims came to Massachusetts. The skipper of that first fishing ship, Captain Gosnold, had good luck. He named Cape Cod for the fish he caught near its shore.

Fishing has been important in the Northeast ever since the days of Captain Gosnold. Many a town on the New England coast began as a fishing community. Boston, Portland, New Bedford, and Gloucester all were early fishing centers.

Oysters are raised like a farm crop in Chesapeake Bay. Here they are being harvested by dredging.

Fish is prepared for market in modern, sanitary packing plants like this one.

Gloucester is still almost completely a fishing town. There you will see fishing boats tied so closely together that you can walk from the deck of one boat to the next. Nets are drying in the sun. And packing and freezing plants crowd together around the harbor.

The ways of fishing are changing. Trim fishing schooners are being replaced by steam trawlers that actually scoop fish from the sea. The hard work of pulling in the nets is now done by heavy machinery. This machinery has replaced crew members, too. Fishing boats today carry a crew of seven. They used to carry 15 to 20 men.

Sound waves are sent out by depth finders from the trawler. These sound waves bounce off schools of fish. They tell the fishermen the exact location of the fish. There is little guesswork in modern fishing. The crew keeps in close touch with their home port. Radio telephones and radio receivers aboard the trawlers give the captain and crew the latest market information and weather reports.

Colorful fishing boats crowd the docks at New Bedford, Mass., once the world's greatest whaling port.

USDA

Unusually fertile soils plus careful farming methods have made southeastern Pennsylvania one of the United States' most prosperous agricultural regions. Farmers have tilled this soil for 250 years.

Farming in the Northeast

Many people live in the Northeast. It takes a lot of food to feed them. Some of the food comes from other parts of the United States. Some even comes from other countries. But some of it comes from northeastern farms.

This Maine potato farmer is spraying his plants. Maine produces more potatoes than any other state.

E. J. Cyr—Shostal

The Northeast is usually thought of as a great industrial workshop. Sometimes we forget about its farms.

Here is a northeastern states Sunday dinner. It will help remind you of some of the good food that comes from northeastern farms.

Tomato juice from Maryland
Frying chicken from Delaware, or
Roasting chicken from Rhode Island, or
Lamb from New Hampshire
Potatoes from Maine
Fresh frozen vegetables from New Jersey
Mushrooms from Pennsylvania
Cranberries from Massachusetts
Milk from Vermont
        and
Apples, peaches, and grapes from New York.

Massachusetts cranberry bogs glow red at harvest time. This state leads in cranberry production.

Much of New England's land is rough and stony. The growing season is short. So many farmers raise dairy cattle. Green pastures, fields of hay, and red barns make a typical New England farm scene.

There is one area of the Northeast where many crops are grown. That is a narrow strip of land along the Atlantic coast, which stretches south from Long Island through Delaware and Maryland.

The sandy soil of this plain is easy to cultivate. There is plenty of rain. The growing season lasts at least six months.

Huge fields of garden vegetables dot the landscape. Some of the vegetables are rushed from the fields in fast trucks to the markets of nearby cities. Some of them go to large canneries. But today many vegetables are carried fresh from the fields to freezing plants, where they are washed, packaged, and frozen within minutes of the time they are picked.

New Jersey specializes in raising vegetables for nearby cities. Here onions are bagged for sale.

These snowy-white Long Island ducks will provide good eating for people all over the United States.

David Lawlor—Shostal

Herbert Lanks—Shostal

Paul Hogan—Shostal

MIDWESTERN UNITED STATES

© State Capitals

Miles
0   100   200

© Copyright 1960 by Map Projects Inc.

Legend:
CHICAGO — Over 1,000,000 population
Columbus — 250,000-1,000,000 population
Flint — 100,000-250,000 population
Sioux Falls — 50,000-100,000 population
Joplin — Under 50,000 population

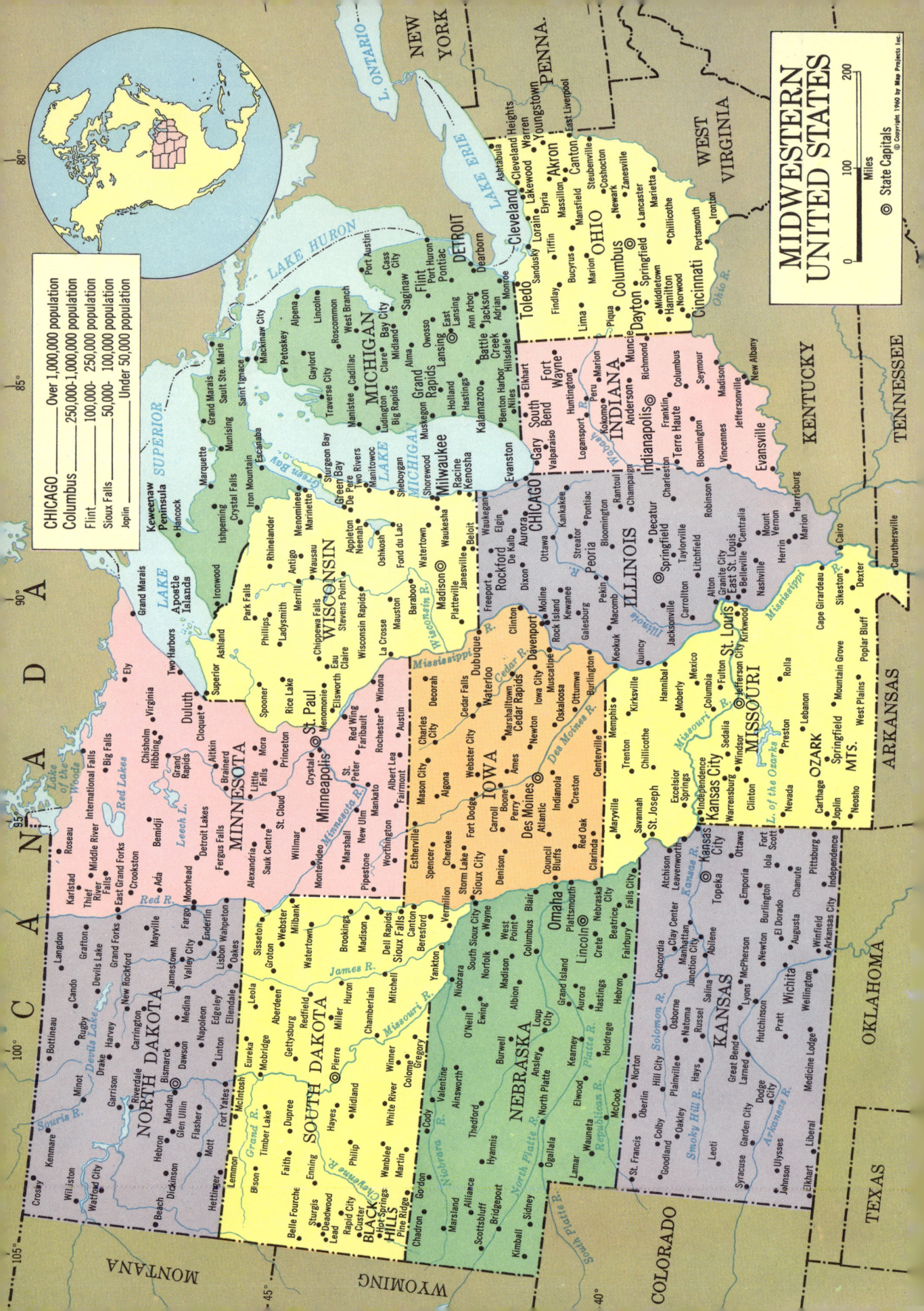

Bodies of Water
LAKE ONTARIO · LAKE ERIE · LAKE HURON · LAKE SUPERIOR · LAKE MICHIGAN · Green Bay · Apostle Islands · Lake of the Woods · Leech L. · Red Lakes · Red R. · Devils Lake · Souris R. · James R. · Missouri R. · Cheyenne R. · Grand R. · Niobrara R. · North Platte R. · South Platte R. · Republican R. · Smoky Hill R. · Solomon R. · Arkansas R. · Platte R. · Loup R. · Kansas R. · Mississippi R. · Minnesota R. · Wisconsin R. · Cedar R. · Des Moines R. · Missouri R. · L. of the Ozarks · Ohio R. · Wabash R. · Illinois R.

States and Provinces
CANADA · NEW YORK · PENNA. · WEST VIRGINIA · KENTUCKY · TENNESSEE · ARKANSAS · OKLAHOMA · TEXAS · COLORADO · WYOMING · MONTANA

NORTH DAKOTA · SOUTH DAKOTA · MINNESOTA · WISCONSIN · MICHIGAN · OHIO · INDIANA · ILLINOIS · IOWA · NEBRASKA · KANSAS · MISSOURI

Selected Cities

Ohio: Cleveland · Cleveland Heights · Lakewood · Lorain · Elyria · Akron · Canton · Massillon · Youngstown · Warren · Steubenville · East Liverpool · Ashtabula · Sandusky · Tiffin · Findlay · Lima · Bucyrus · Marion · Mansfield · Mount Vernon · Newark · Zanesville · Coshocton · Lancaster · Marietta · Columbus · Springfield · Dayton · Middletown · Hamilton · Norwood · Cincinnati · Chillicothe · Portsmouth · Ironton · Piqua · Toledo

Michigan: Detroit · Dearborn · Pontiac · Flint · Saginaw · Bay City · Midland · Lansing · East Lansing · Jackson · Ann Arbor · Adrian · Monroe · Port Huron · Battle Creek · Kalamazoo · Grand Rapids · Muskegon · Holland · Benton Harbor · Niles · Flint · Owosso · Alma · Clare · Cadillac · Traverse City · Manistee · Ludington · Big Rapids · Gaylord · Petoskey · Roscommon · West Branch · Alpena · Lincoln · Cass City · Port Austin · Mackinaw City · Saint Ignace · Sault Ste. Marie · Grand Marais · Munising · Marquette · Escanaba · Menominee · Iron Mountain · Crystal Falls · Ishpeming · Hancock · Two Rivers · Sheboygan

Indiana: Indianapolis · Fort Wayne · South Bend · Gary · Hammond · Muncie · Anderson · Richmond · Marion · Kokomo · Peru · Logansport · Huntington · Valparaiso · Elkhart · Terre Haute · Bloomington · Vincennes · Evansville · New Albany · Jeffersonville · Madison · Columbus · Franklin · Seymour · Charleston

Illinois: Chicago · Evanston · Waukegan · Elgin · Aurora · Joliet · Rockford · Freeport · De Kalb · Dixon · Rock Island · Moline · Kewanee · Galesburg · Peoria · Pekin · Macomb · Quincy · Jacksonville · Springfield · Decatur · Bloomington · Champaign · Rantoul · Kankakee · Pontiac · Streator · Ottawa · Taylorville · Litchfield · Alton · Granite City · East St. Louis · Belleville · Nashville · Centralia · Mount Vernon · Marion · Herrin · Cairo · Robinson · Carrollton

Wisconsin: Milwaukee · Racine · Kenosha · Waukesha · Madison · Beloit · Janesville · Watertown · Fond du Lac · Oshkosh · Appleton · Neenah · Sheboygan · Manitowoc · Green Bay · De Pere · Sturgeon Bay · Marinette · Wausau · Antigo · Rhinelander · Merrill · Stevens Point · Wisconsin Rapids · Baraboo · Mauston · Portage · La Crosse · Eau Claire · Chippewa Falls · Ladysmith · Phillips · Park Falls · Ironwood · Ashland · Superior · Spooner · Rice Lake

Minnesota: Minneapolis · St. Paul · Duluth · Cloquet · Hibbing · Chisholm · Virginia · Ely · Grand Rapids · Brainerd · Aitkin · Bemidji · Crookston · East Grand Forks · Ada · Moorhead · Fergus Falls · Detroit Lakes · Alexandria · Sauk Centre · Willmar · St. Cloud · Little Falls · Mora · Princeton · Montevideo · Marshall · New Ulm · Mankato · St. Peter · Faribault · Red Wing · Winona · Rochester · Austin · Albert Lea · Fairmont · Worthington · Pipestone · Crystal · International Falls · Big Falls · Roseau · Karlstad · Thief River Falls · Middle River · Grand Forks · Grand Marais · Two Harbors

Iowa: Des Moines · Cedar Rapids · Davenport · Waterloo · Dubuque · Iowa City · Muscatine · Burlington · Ottumwa · Oskaloosa · Newton · Marshalltown · Ames · Boone · Fort Dodge · Webster City · Mason City · Charles City · Decorah · Cedar Falls · Clinton · Keokuk · Centerville · Indianola · Creston · Red Oak · Atlantic · Council Bluffs · Clarinda · Sioux City · Denison · Storm Lake · Cherokee · Spencer · Estherville · Algona · Carroll · Perry

Nebraska: Omaha · Lincoln · Plattsmouth · Nebraska City · Beatrice · Fairbury · Crete · Blair · Fremont · Columbus · West Point · Norfolk · Madison · Wayne · South Sioux City · Grand Island · Hastings · Aurora · Albion · Hebron · Geneva · Kearney · Holdrege · Elwood · North Platte · Ogallala · Sidney · Bridgeport · Scottsbluff · Kimball · Alliance · Chadron · Gordon · Valentine · Ainsworth · O'Neill · Burwell · Ansley · Loup City · Broken Bow · Thedford · Hyannis · Cody · Niobrara · Ewing

South Dakota: Pierre · Sioux Falls · Watertown · Aberdeen · Brookings · Madison · Huron · Mitchell · Yankton · Vermillion · Chamberlain · Gregory · Winner · Colome · White River · Midland · Philip · Wall · Martin · Pine Ridge · Hot Springs · Rapid City · Custer · Deadwood · Lead · Sturgis · Belle Fourche · Newell · Faith · Timber Lake · Mobridge · Gettysburg · Redfield · Miller · Eureka · McIntosh · Bison · Lemmon · Dupree · Hayes · Wanblee · Groton · Sisseton · Milbank · Webster

North Dakota: Bismarck · Mandan · Fargo · Grand Forks · Jamestown · Valley City · Devils Lake · Minot · Williston · Dickinson · Mott · Hettinger · Beach · Watford City · New Rockford · Carrington · Harvey · Rugby · Rolla · Cando · Langdon · Grafton · Mayville · Cooperstown · Casselton · Wahpeton · Lisbon · Oakes · Ellendale · Edgeley · Napoleon · Linton · Fort Yates · Garrison · Washburn · Riverdale · Glen Ullin · Flasher · Hebron · Bottineau · Kenmare · Crosby · Drake · Enderlin

Kansas: Topeka · Kansas City · Wichita · Hutchinson · Salina · Manhattan · Junction City · Emporia · Lawrence · Leavenworth · Atchison · Ottawa · Fort Scott · Pittsburg · Iola · Chanute · Independence · Arkansas City · Winfield · El Dorado · Newton · McPherson · Lyons · Great Bend · Larned · Pratt · Dodge City · Garden City · Syracuse · Ulysses · Johnson · Elkhart · Liberal · Meade · Medicine Lodge · Wellington · Augusta · Burlington · Concordia · Clay Center · Osborne · Natoma · Russell · Hays · Norton · Oberlin · Colby · Oakley · Goodland · St. Francis · Leoti · Hill City · Plainville

Missouri: St. Louis · Kansas City · Jefferson City · Springfield · Columbia · Independence · St. Joseph · Sedalia · Hannibal · Joplin · Cape Girardeau · Sikeston · Poplar Bluff · Dexter · Caruthersville · Rolla · Lebanon · Mountain Grove · West Plains · Nevada · Carthage · Neosho · Mexico · Fulton · Moberly · Kirksville · Chillicothe · Trenton · Maryville · Savannah · Excelsior Springs · Windsor · Clinton · Preston · Warrensburg · Memphis

Physical Features
Keweenaw Peninsula · Black Hills · Ozark Mts. · L. of the Ozarks

In Illinois broad fields of corn provide farmers with their most valued cash crop.

Max Burk—Black Star

THE MIDWEST

No other farm region in the world equals the Midwest in food production or in the prosperity of its farmers. More people in the Midwest work in factories than on farms. But farming is certainly the Midwest's leading industry. With their large farms, and with machinery, midwestern farmers are more than able to meet the food needs of the country.

Here is just part of the share of the United States' farm products that are grown in the Midwest—nine tenths of the soybeans, three fifths of the wheat, four fifths of the corn, seven eighths of the swine, and three fifths of all livestock.

The eastern portion of the Midwest is corn country. This region is often called the Corn Belt. Ohio, Indiana, Illinois, Iowa, Nebraska, Kansas, and Missouri are leading Corn Belt states.

Corn is the pioneer American crop. It was certainly one of the first crops grown on American farms. The Indians taught the early settlers how to grow it.

As pioneers began to move westward, corn moved with them. In the Midwest these pioneers found an ideal climate for growing corn.

USDA

Feeder farms for beef cattle, like these Hereford steers, are a specialty of the Corn Belt.

USDA

These pigs are turning corn into meat.

Corn likes hot summer days. It likes hot nights too. Corn also likes plenty of summer rain. If the weather is hot, and the rains fall, corn will sometimes grow an inch or more in a day.

Midwestern corn often goes to market "on the hoof." Some farmers sell their corn in town, but most feed it to hogs and cattle. Farmers can make more money from fat hogs and fat cattle than they can from selling their corn directly.

Corn is not the only crop grown in the Corn Belt. Actually it is grown on less than half of the cropland. More than half of the cropland is used for hay, soybeans, oats, and wheat. But, like corn, these are crops that can be fed to livestock.

The patterns of plowed fields show clearly in this aerial view of typical midwestern farming country.

USDA

A. M. Wettach—Shostal

Well-managed dairy farms like this make Wisconsin's farmers prosperous.

Chester Kronfeld—FPG

The northern portion of the Midwest is a hay and dairy region. Here the long, cold winters and cool, moist summers discourage the growing of corn. But these conditions are just right for growing hay. And hay makes fine feed for dairy cattle.

Wisconsin is the leading dairy state. Most of Wisconsin's milk is made into cheese and butter. Nearly half of the cheese made in the United States comes from Wisconsin.

The drier western portions of the Midwest are wheat lands. From the Dakotas southward to Oklahoma is wheat country. Here farms are huge, and there are few towns. You can drive for miles and see nothing but wheat, wheat, and more wheat.

Feed, oil, and plastics are but a few of the varied products yielded by soybeans.

To Buffalo's busy harbor, lake ships bring heavy
cargoes of midwestern grain and ore.

Grain is stored in huge elevators at flour mills of
General Mills in Minneapolis, Minnesota.

Industry in the Midwest

The Midwest has what it takes to be a
great manufacturing center. What are
these requirements for manufacturing?

First, there must be a big supply of
power. The Midwest has tremendous quantities of coal. Oil and natural gas are available, too.

Secondly, there must be a good supply
and variety of raw materials. The Midwest

has them—iron ore, livestock, wheat, and
timber are just a few.

There must be plenty of workers. Money
has to be available to build factories. There
must be a good transportation network.
And, finally, there must be a good market
for the products. The Midwest has no
trouble meeting all of these requirements.

For many years the processing of food
products ranked first among the Midwest's
manufactures. But today machinery, metal
products, and automobiles have taken the
lead. However, meat packing and flour milling are still big midwestern businesses.

Years ago almost all slaughtering and
meat packing was done on the farms where
the livestock was raised. But fast transportation and refrigeration now bring the
animals to huge packing plants in large
midwestern cities. These meat packers find
a use for almost every part of the animal.
One packer in Chicago says he uses every
part of the pig except the squeal.

In the refrigeration rooms of meat-packing plants,
government inspectors grade the meat.

The steel industry's demand for iron ore created this large mine in Minnesota's Mesabi range.

Ewing Galloway

Good transportation is important in flour milling, as well. Railroads deliver tons of wheat to mills in Minneapolis, Kansas City, St. Louis, and Wichita. Buffalo, at the eastern end of Lake Erie in New York State, is an even greater milling center. It is cheaper to transport goods by water than by rail; so every year huge grain ships deliver their cargoes of midwestern wheat to the flour mills of Buffalo.

Cheap water transportation made possible the growth of an important iron and steel industry along the shores of the lower Great Lakes. Specially-built boats carry iron ore hundreds of miles from the mines of Minnesota, Wisconsin, and northern Michigan to the steel mills of such cities as Gary, Indiana. At night the sky glows red from the huge blast furnaces. Coal and limestone, also needed for producing iron and steel, come from nearby mines and quarries.

The iron and steel industry of the lower Great Lakes will probably become even more important since the United States and Canada have completed the St. Lawrence Seaway. Now ocean-going ships can sail 2,347 miles—all the way from the Gulf of the St. Lawrence on the Atlantic Ocean, to Duluth, at the western end of Lake Superior. This means that ships can bring huge loads of iron ore from the rich new mines in Labrador to the blast furnaces of the Midwest.

An ore boat arrives at the unloading docks of the U.S. Steel plant at Gary, Indiana.

Van Bucher—Photo Researchers

56

Ewing Galloway

Detroit's automobile factories operate night and day. The automobile industry is the largest steel user.

When you hear "Detroit," you think of automobiles. It is the center of the Midwest's greatest industry. Over half the motor vehicles and equipment made in the United States come from the Midwest. And over two fifths come from Michigan alone.

Workmen place the body shell on an automobile chassis in this River Rouge, Michigan, factory.

Courtesy of the Ford Motor Company

Mild winters and abundant sunshine and rainfall make Florida a great citrus-growing state.

THE SOUTH

Most of the South is a land of long, hot summers. Winters are short and cool. There is abundant rainfall. This combination gives the South a long growing season. And the long growing season has helped make the South a great farming region.

In the past the story of southern farming has been the story of three crops—cotton, tobacco, and corn. Cotton and tobacco were the cash crops. This means that the farmer grew them to sell. Corn was raised to provide food for the farmer's family and his livestock.

Cotton, tobacco, and corn hurt southern farmers. All three are row crops—planted in straight lines. All of the weeds have to

Early fruit production is a southern specialty.

Tobacco is dried before being further processed.

SOUTHERN UNITED STATES

◎ State Capitals

Symbol	Population
New Orleans	250,000–1,000,000 population
Savannah	100,000– 250,000 population
San Angelo	50,000– 100,000 population
Fredericksburg	Under 50,000 population

Miles

0   100   200   300

© Copyright 1960 by Map Projects, Inc.

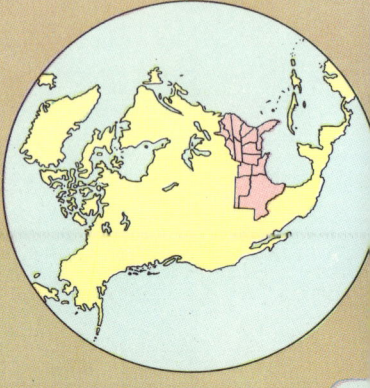

Mechanical cotton-pickers are replacing hand labor in the cottonfields of the South.

USDA

be cleared between the rows. This means that no vegetation is left to hold the soil in place during heavy rains. And the South does have heavy rains.

During a summer thundershower, rainwater rushed across open fields, carrying away tons of good soil. In some places this washing away of the soil caused great gullies to form. When this happened the farmland had to be abandoned.

Big changes are taking place on southern farms. Farmers are working hard to improve their soil. Plenty of fertilizer is being used. And the farmers are plowing their fields in ways that help keep the soil in place.

Cotton, tobacco, and corn have not been forgotten. But other crops have been added to the southern farm scene. Peanuts and soybeans are both important southern cash crops now. And they are crops that help to improve the soil as well as to add cash to the farmer's pockets.

The greatest change in southern farming is the growth of the beef-cattle industry. Abandoned cotton land has been changed to ranch land. Some southern ranches are larger than those in the West. The mild southern winters mean year-round green pastures. The South is fast becoming the new home of the cowboy.

Texas, long famous for cowpunchers and cattle, still leads the United States in livestock production.

Bob Taylor—FPG

Closeness to raw materials, abundant and cheap fuel supplies, and a good location on the Gulf Coast . . . all these combine to make Houston a North American leader in the processing and shipping of chemicals.

The South's Growing Industries

The South is rich in natural resources. This natural wealth is helping to build new industries in a land where farming has always ruled. Here is some of the natural wealth that is available in the South:

Think first about minerals.

Sulfur and salt are found in great domes along the western Gulf Coast in Louisiana and Texas. Seven tenths of the world's supply of sulfur, and the entire United States supply, comes from this region. There are enormous quantities of salt, too. Sulfur and salt form the basis for a growing southern chemical industry.

Phosphate rock is another important southern mineral. Phosphate is used in making fertilizer. Most plants need large quantities of phosphate fertilizer to grow well. Most of the phosphate mined in the United States comes from the Gulf side of central Florida. Some comes from Tennessee. The Florida phosphate mines alone can keep the farmers of the United States supplied for the next 4,000 years.

Phosphate rock is mined in Florida. The rock is blasted loose by high-pressure jets of water.

Bauxite, the ore of aluminum, is widely scattered over the South. More than nine tenths of the bauxite mined in the United States comes from central Arkansas.

There are great supplies of iron ore in the South, although it is mined only in a few places. Most of the iron ore is mined near Birmingham, Alabama. One mountain there has a seam of iron ore more than 25 miles in length. This ore has helped make Birmingham an important producer of iron and steel.

Think now of power resources — coal, oil, natural gas, and water power.

Billions of barrels of oil lie under Southern plains and swamps, and there are billions more under the waters of the Gulf of Mexico. At least one third of the natural gas reserves and one fourth of the oil reserves in the United States are in the South. Oil and natural gas are helping a great new refinery and chemical industry to develop in the South.

B. A. Lang, Sr.—Shostal

Refining petroleum is one of the leading industries in the South. Huge oil refineries dotting the landscape are a common sight.

Oilfields, like these, produce crude oil which must then be processed at a refinery.

Fred Bond—FPG

Sulfur from nearby Gulf Coast mines is loaded onto a ship in Galveston harbor.

Frank E. Meitz—Shostal

Herbert Lanks—Black Star

Granite quarries like this are abundant in Georgia.

Jerry Cooke—Photo Researchers

Birmingham is the South's leading steel producer.

What about coal? Southern coal mines produce two fifths of the United States' coal. Most of it is shipped to the northern states. Southern industry uses more natural gas and electricity than coal to supply its power.

The South has what is needed for water power—mountains down which streams can pour, and plenty of rainfall. The southern highlands are a major source of the

water power of the United States. Many dams have been built to convert southern water power to electricity.

Finally, think about timber.

More than half of the southern landscape is covered with forests. Two fifths of the country's timber comes from the South. More than half of the pulp and one third of the paper of the United States come out of the southern states. With its long growing season and heavy rainfall, the South has an ideal forest climate. The future looks bright for southern industries that depend upon forest products.

Sap from southern pines is used to make such products as tar and turpentine.

Robert Thomas—Camera Clix

Spaniards planted the first wheat in California. Today it occupies a large portion of the cropland.

Ripening oranges cover the neatly spaced trees of this scientifically managed California grove.

USDA

THE WEST

Few places in the world have such a variety of ways of using the land as the West. Water often determines how the land will be used. In only a few portions of the West is water available in quantities large enough for farming.

There are vast areas of desert. But there are places where enough rain falls to allow scrub plants to grow. There huge livestock ranches are found. The natural vegetation is so sparse that it may take more than 120 acres just to support one steer. In country like that some ranches have more than half a million acres.

Sheep ranchers also use the dry lands. Sheep can browse on leaves, weeds, and woody plants which cattle will not eat. So sheep can live on parts of the western land where cattle cannot get along.

Josef Muench

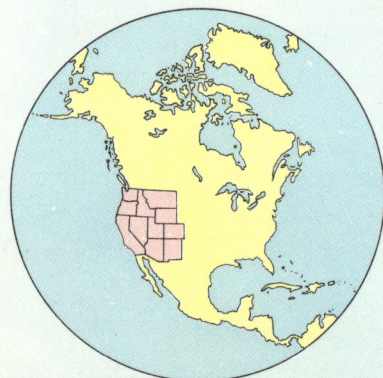

WESTERN UNITED STATES

CANADA

MEXICO

TEXAS

NORTH DAKOTA
SOUTH DAKOTA
NEBRASKA
KANSAS
OKLA.

WASHINGTON
OREGON
CALIFORNIA
NEVADA
IDAHO
MONTANA
WYOMING
UTAH
COLORADO
ARIZONA
NEW MEXICO

PACIFIC OCEAN
GULF OF CALIFORNIA

◎ State Capitals

0   100   200   300
Miles

LOS ANGELES —— Over 1,000,000 population
Portland —— 250,000–1,000,000 population
Phoenix —— 100,000–250,000 population
Bakersfield —— 50,000–100,000 population
Roswell —— Under 50,000 population

© Copyright 1960 by Map Projects Inc.

In the spring, sheep are driven high into western mountains to seek fresh, green pastures.

The opposite of the huge western ranch is the small irrigated farm. Where water is available, green patches appear on the brown desert. These green patches are valuable. On them are grown fine crops of vegetables, melons, and fruit.

The three states of the West Coast— California, Oregon, and Washington — have important farm lands. But there is a great difference in the kinds of crops produced in central and southern California and the farm lands to the north.

Spaniards and Mexicans were California's first farmers. They used the land to graze great herds of cattle.

California became part of the United States in 1845. When gold was discovered four years later, California's population grew rapidly, and more food was needed. The huge ranches of the old days were divided into smaller farms. Wheat soon became the chief crop. Rice and barley became important too. Today four fifths

Idaho is famous for its potatoes. Modern methods of irrigation ensure a good crop every year.

This cotton was grown near Tucson, Arizona. Irrigation turned desert into fertile farmland.

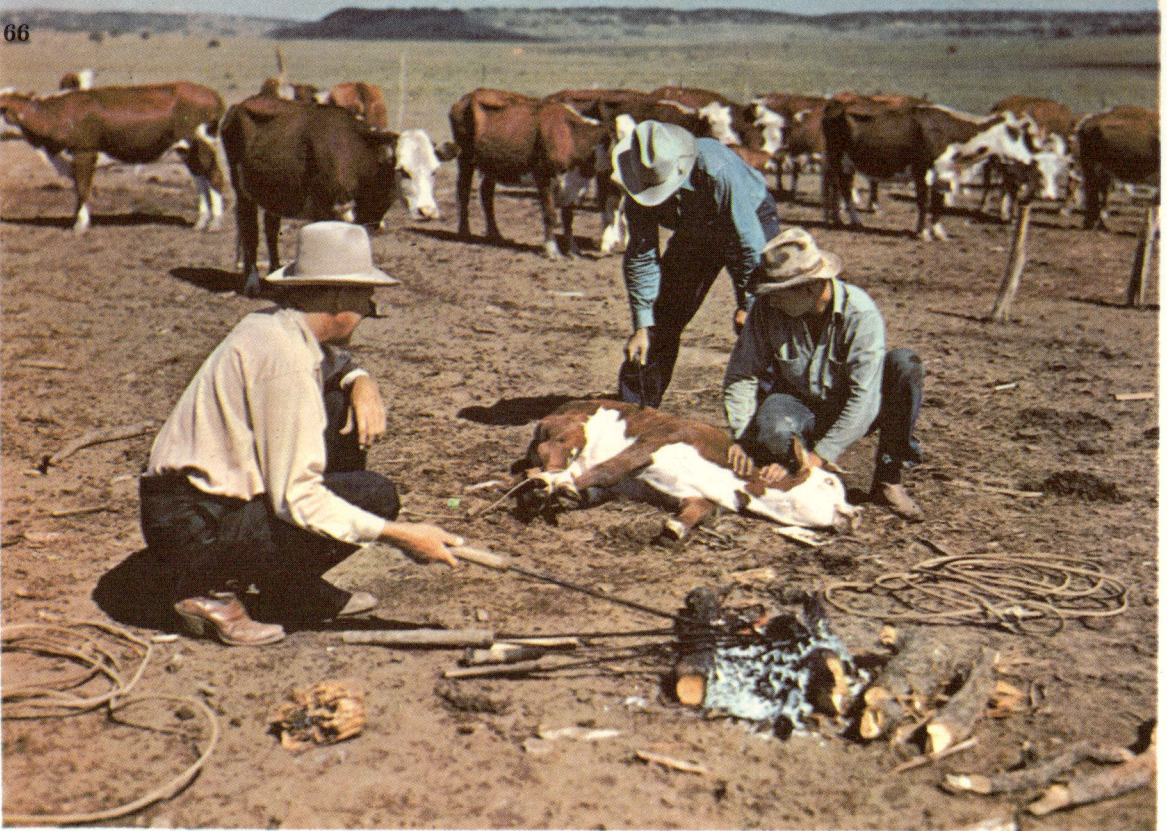

Cattle branding is a busy time on western ranches. Brands help distinguish cattle from different herds.

of California's cropland is still used for grazing and for grains. But other more specialized crops produce nine tenths of

the value of California's farm products. These crops are cotton, vegetables, fruits, nuts, and dairy products.

California is now the country's second most important cotton-producing state. Only Texas grows more cotton. And California farmers also grow half of the country's fruits and vegetables.

Farms of western Washington and Oregon have no water shortage problem. Plenty of rain falls there. This is also a region with mild winters and cool summers. It is ideal dairy country. More than four fifths of the cropland is used for hay, grains for feed, and pasture.

Poultry and eggs are also important in the northwestern portion of the United States. And nearly all of the country's flax used for fiber is grown in Oregon's Willamette Valley. Flax fiber is used in making linen cloth.

Washington and Oregon are large fruit-growing states. This is a Washington cherry orchard.

The Industrial West

In the western mountain states no industry is more important than mining. More than half of the workers of this region earn their living in the mineral industries.

Mining began in the mountain country 100 years ago. At first miners were interested only in gold and silver. They had little use for the copper, lead, and zinc that they found with the gold and silver ore. Copper, lead, and zinc did not seem valuable enough to go to the expense of processing the ore. Then scientists found less expensive methods of processing these ores. Today copper, lead, and zinc are more important than gold and silver in the mountain states.

The West Coast is growing fast. By 1970 California will probably have more people than any of the 50 states. Thousands of families are also moving to Washington and Oregon.

Plenty of jobs are waiting for skilled workers in modern west coast factories. The center of west coast manufacturing is the Los Angeles area. Only New York, Chicago, Detroit, and Philadelphia have more industrial workers than Los Angeles.

Seventy years ago Los Angeles was a farm community. Then oil was discovered. Oil brought manufacturing to this region.

D. Horter—FPG

In the Pacific Northwest, salmon rank first in value among the fish resources.

Arizona is famous for its mineral resources. Its production of copper leads all the other states'.

Bill Sears—Black Star

L. Willinger—FPG

Hollywood has been the world's motion-picture capital for more than half a century.

Ralph Luce—Shostal

Fruit and vegetable packing is a major California industry. These workers are grading strawberries.

Courtesy of the Boeing Airplane Company

Huge aircraft factories in California and Washington produce modern jet airplanes.

Gene Larmon

In 1909 the first movie studio opened in Los Angeles. Today the whole world looks to the Los Angeles suburb, Hollywood, for movies. In recent years it also has become a television center.

But it was World War II that really made Los Angeles a great manufacturing center. Aircraft manufacturing became the chief industry. Automobile assembly plants, tire manufacturing, and the sewing of sport clothes also employ thousands of workers in the Los Angeles area.

Another great west coast manufacturing center is the San Francisco Bay area. The fine harbor and port facilities have attracted many industries. Food processing and oil refining have long been important in this area. And now electronics is an important new industry.

The Pacific Northwest is the third west coast manufacturing center. Seattle, Tacoma, and Portland are the chief cities. The Northwest's natural wealth—timber, fish, and wheat—is processed and shipped to markets around the world.

This northern California sawmill is representative of the Pacific Coast's great lumber industry.

HAWAII

Here is the "Paradise of the Pacific." Perhaps you know it better as the state of Hawaii. But the pleasant climate, blue Pacific Ocean, towering green mountains, and fine beaches make the Hawaiian Islands seem like "paradise" to many a visitor.

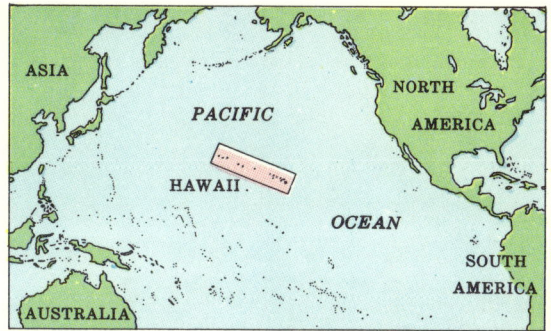

Honolulu, Hawaii's capital, is at the "crossroads of the Pacific Ocean." Many ships sailing between Asia and North America stop at Honolulu's fine harbor. And airplanes heading for Japan, China, the Philippine Islands, Australia, and New Zealand stop at Honolulu's airport to refuel. If you look at a map of the Pacific Ocean you will see why Honolulu is at the "crossroads of the Pacific."

Hawaii's first settlers were brown-skinned Polynesian people. They sailed their outrigger canoes northward from the islands of the South Pacific hundreds of years before the first white men sailed those waters.

Today there are few pure-blooded Polynesians left in the Hawaiian Islands. People from all over the world have flocked to the islands—Japanese, Chinese, Koreans, Filipinos, Puerto Ricans, Europeans, and people from the mainland United States.

Few places in the world have a population with such a variety of races living happily together.

Hawaii has two main industries—growing sugar cane and pineapples. These two crops use more than nine tenths of the Hawaiian Islands' cropland.

No crops in the world are grown more scientifically than Hawaiian sugar cane and pineapples. Skilled scientists are always at work seeking better ways of producing these crops.

Hawaii's "third industry" is taking care of tourists. Fine hotels line the famous beaches. Mountain scenery and active volcanoes are exciting attractions. The Hawaii National Park is famed for its fiery volcano Mauna Loa. And the year-round warm waters and sunny climate have special tourist appeal.

Lumahai Beach, on the island of Kauai, shows why Hawaii is a popular vacation land.

Ray Atkeson

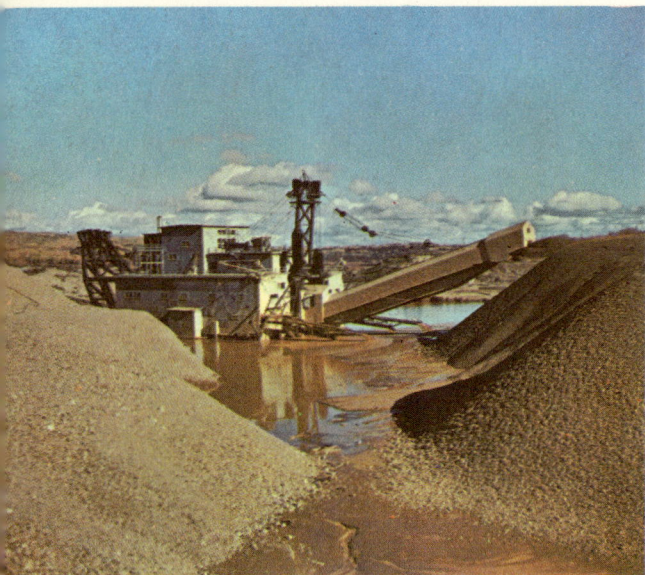

Charles C. Ray—Shostal

Where prospectors once panned for gold, today large dredges scoop up gold-bearing gravel from the Yukon River basin near Fairbanks.

Alaskan king crabs, like these taken from the cold waters of the Bering Sea, sometimes measure four feet across and are considered a great delicacy.

Bob and Ira Spring

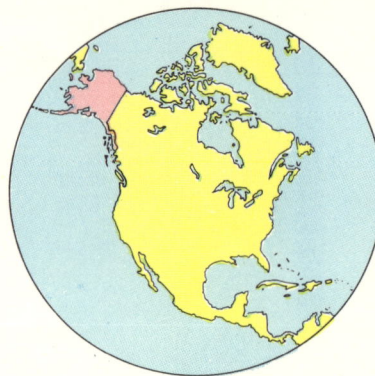

ALASKA

One hundred years ago Alaska was Russian territory. The United States purchased Alaska from Russia in 1867. The price was less than two cents an acre. But even at that price many people thought that the United States had been cheated. They thought of Alaska as a land suited only for Eskimos.

We know better today. Each year enough gold is mined in Alaska to more than pay the price given to the Russians. And the value of the fish caught in Alaskan waters is even greater than the value of Alaska's gold. There are great stores of oil and timber in Alaska that have scarcely been touched.

But even if Alaska had no natural wealth at all, it would still be important to the United States. Look at Alaska's position on a globe. Alaska is only a few miles from the Soviet Union. Fairbanks is almost as close to Moscow as it is to Chicago. Military men say that Alaska has a strategic location. This means that its position is important in defending the rest of the United States. The Armed Forces have many men, airplanes, and ships in Alaska.

Alaska is an air-age state. A larger portion of people fly and own planes than in any other state. A look at the map or the globe again tells why Alaska is huge. There are few roads or railroads. Places are far apart. If you want to travel anyplace in Alaska except along the coast, you fly.

Snow-capped Mt. Popocatepetl rises nearly 18,000 feet above sea level. It is Mexico's second-highest mountain. Once an active volcano, it still at times emits vast clouds of smoke.

MEXICO, LAND OF CONTRASTS

Mexico has something of almost everything. Think first about the land. Two thirds of Mexico is mountainous. Slopes are so steep that the people do not think of east, west, north, or south when they travel. They think of "up" and "down."

The other one third of Mexico is a lowland. Here are narrow valleys, broad basins, swampy coasts, and a wide limestone plain with underground rivers.

Or think about climate. To the south there is a wet Mexico. Part of this region is a land of tropical rain forests. But to the north there are deserts.

Parts of Mexico are so high that even the summers are cool. But in the lowlands people swelter in the summer heat.

Think about people. There is an empty Mexico. You might travel for miles across the dry lands and never see a person or a house. But there is also a crowded Mexico. Most of Mexico's people live in the central highland around Mexico City. Mexico City is one of the largest cities in the world. Only eight other cities, including Tokyo, London, and New York are larger.

Or think about the past. Few countries have a more exciting history.

In 1519 the first European landed on the Mexican coast. He was Hernando Cortés. Cortés led his men to the capital city of the ruling Indians, the Aztecs.

The Aztec capital was Mexico City. Here was no mere Indian village. This was a real

MEXICO

Miles
0   100   200   300

MEXICO CITY	Over 1,000,000 population
Monterrey	250,000-1,000,000 population
Mérida	100,000- 250,000 population
Chihuahua	50,000- 100,000 population
San Luis	Under 50,000 population

◉ National Capital

© Copyright 1960 by Map Projects Inc.

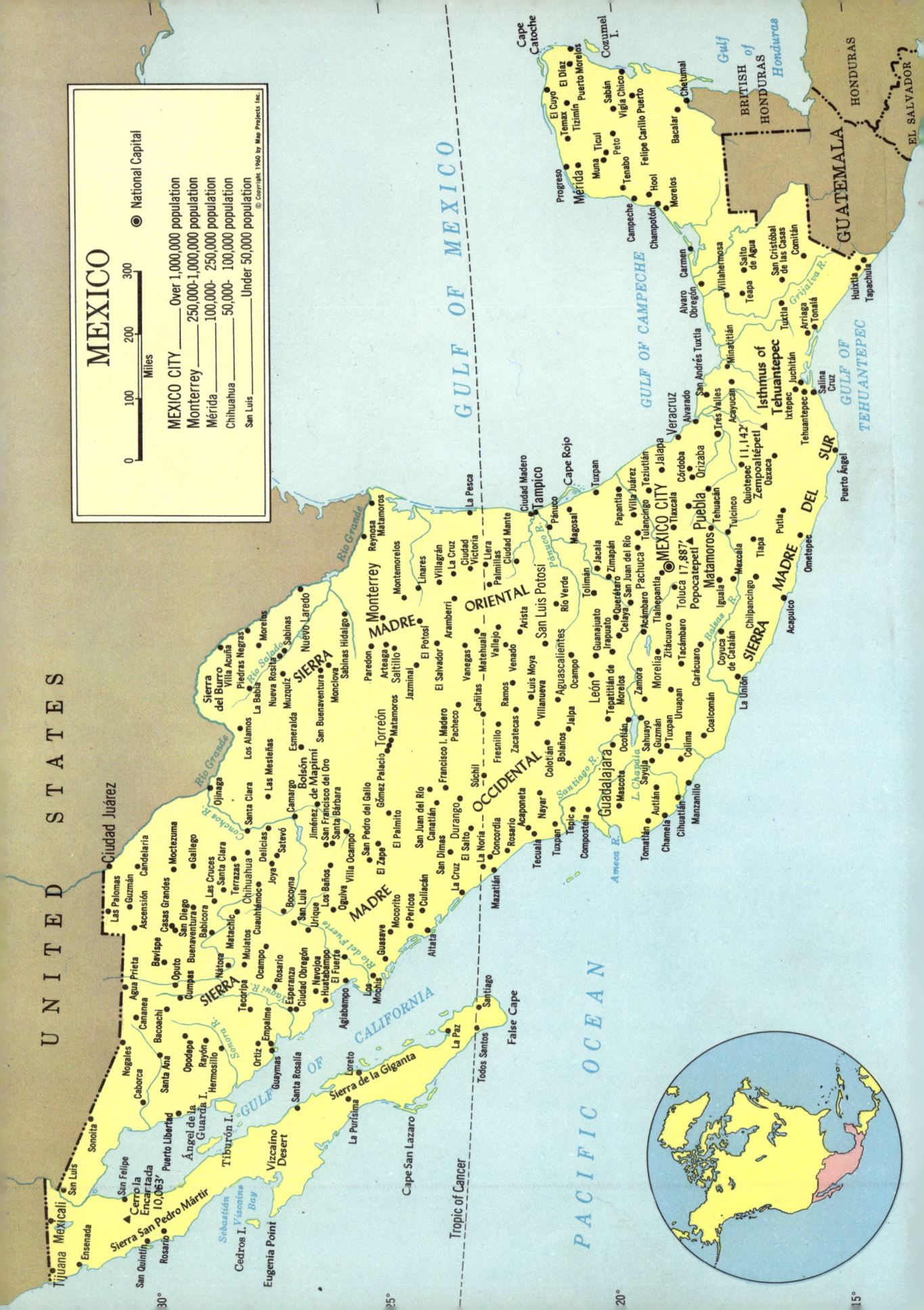

GULF OF MEXICO

GULF OF CAMPECHE

GULF OF TEHUANTEPEC

PACIFIC OCEAN

GULF OF CALIFORNIA

UNITED STATES

GUATEMALA

BRITISH HONDURAS

HONDURAS

EL SALVADOR

Gulf of Honduras

Cape Catoche
Cozumel I.
El Diaz
Puerto Morelos
El Cuyo
Temax
Tizimín
Sabán
Vigia Chico Puerto
Muna
Ticul
Peto
Tenabo
Hool
Morelos
Bacalar
Chetumal
Felipe Carillo Puerto
Progreso
Mérida
Campeche
Champotón
Alvaro
Carmen
Obregón
Villahermosa
Salto de Agua
San Cristóbal de las Casas
Comitán
Teapa
Tuxtla
Arriaga
Tonalá
Huixtla
Tapachula
Minatitlán
San Andrés Tuxtla
Tres Valles
Acayucan
Ixtepec
Juchitán
Salina Cruz
Tehuantepec
Isthmus of Tehuantepec

Cape Rojo
Ciudad Madero
Tampico
Pánuco
Tuxpan
Magosal
Papantla
Villa Juárez
Tezuitlán
Tulancingo
Pachuca
Jalapa
Córdoba
Orizaba
Veracruz
Alvarado
Quiotepec 11,142
Zempoaltépetl ▲
Oaxaca
Puebla
Tehuacán
Popocatepetl ▲ 17,887
MEXICO CITY ◉
Toluca 17,887 ▲
Matamoros
Mezcalla
Tlapa
Putla
Ometepec
Chilpancingo
Acapulco
Puerto Angel

SIERRA MADRE DEL SUR

SIERRA MADRE ORIENTAL

SIERRA MADRE OCCIDENTAL

La Pesca
Reynosa
Matamoros
Montemorelos
Linares
Villagrán
Ciudad Victoria
Llera
Palmillas
Ciudad Mante
Jacala
Zimapán
Querétaro
San Juan del Río
Celaya
Tlanepantla
Tlaxcala
Tlacámbaro
Amecameca
Iguala
Coyuca de Catalán
La Unión
Coalcomán
Manzanillo
Colima

Monterrey
Morelos
Sabinas
Nuevo Laredo
Paredón
Arteaga
Saltillo
El Potosí
Vanegas
Matehuala
Arista
Venado
Luis Moya
Aguascalientes
Ocampo
León
Guanajuato
Irapuato
Tepatitlán de Morelos
Zamora
Morelia
Uruapan
Tacámbaro
Carácuaro

Sierra del Burro
Villa Acuña
Piedras Negras
La Babia
Nueva Rosita
Muzquiz
Monclova
Sabinas Hidalgo
Jazminal
El Salvador
Cañitas
Ramos
Zacatecas
Villanueva
Jalpa
Bolaños
Colotlán
Tuxpan
Guzmán
Sahuayo
Zitácuaro

Francisco I. Madero
Pacheco
Torreón
Gómez Palacio
Matamoros
Fresnillo
Sóchil
Durango
La Cruz
El Salto
La Noria
Concordia
Rosario
Mazatlán
Acaponeta
Nayar
Tepic
Compostela
Tecuala
Tuxpan
Santiago
Ixcuintla
Guadalajara
Autlán
L. Chapala
Sayula
Mascota
Cihuatlán
Chamela
Tomatlán

Esmeralda
Bolsón de Mapimí
Jiménez
San Francisco del Oro
Santa Bárbara
Los Alamos
Las Mestas
El Zape
El Palmito
San Pedro del Gallo
San Juan del Río
Canatlán
San Dimas

Chihuahua
Joya
Cuauhtémoc
Uríque
Guavas
Los Baños
Guavas
Mocorito
Pericos
Culiacán
Altata

Ojinaga
Santa Clara
Satevó
Bocoyna
San Luis
Delicias
Camargo

Ciudad Juárez
Las Palomas
Ascensión
Candelaria
Guzmán
Casas Grandes
San Diego
Las Cruces
Babicora
Terrazas
Moctezuma
Gallego

Agua Prieta
Bavispe
Oputo
Cumpas
Esperanza
Bacoachi
Cananea
Nogales
Caborca
Santa Ana
Opodepe
Rayón
Hermosillo
Ortiz
Empalme
Guaymas
Santa Rosalía

Mexicali
Tijuana
Ensenada
San Luis
San Felipe
Cerro la Encantada 10,063'
San Pedro Mártir
Rosario
San Quintín
Puerto Libertad
Ángel de la Guarda I.
Tiburón I.
Cedros I. (Cerros I.)
Eugenia Point
Vizcaíno Desert
La Purísima
Loreto
La Paz
Sierra de la Giganta
Todos Santos
Santiago
San José del Cabo
Cape San Lucas
Cape San Lázaro

Río Grande
Rio Salado
Conchos R.
Rio del Fuerte
Santiago R.
Ameca R.
Grijalva R.
Balsas R.
Pánuco R.

Tropic of Cancer

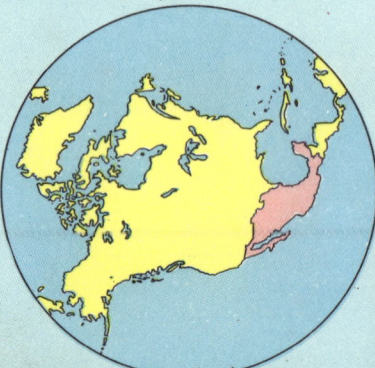

30°   25°   20°   15°

George Hunter—FPG

This ancient pyramid is in the Central Valley of Mexico, where most of Mexico's population lives today.

city. There were fine palaces for the rulers. And, even more wonderful, there were beautiful temples and huge stone pyramids.

The Aztecs were the ruling Indians of Mexico. When they conquered Mexico 200 years before Cortés arrived, two other powerful tribes lived in Mexico. They were the Toltecs and the Mayans. These tribes, too, built temples of stone. They also wove cloth from cotton and made ornaments and tools of gold, silver, and copper.

Aztec, Toltec, and Mayan ruins can still be seen in Mexico. The glory of their works rivals the pyramids of ancient Egypt. Many of the people of Mexico today are descendants of the Indians who built these wonders.

This luxuriant tropical forest is in the state of Nayarit, on Mexico's Pacific coast.

Otto Done—FPG

Much of the world's supply of silver comes from mines like this one in the Mexican highlands.

Mexican Mines and Manufacturing

Dreams of gold and silver brought the first explorers to Mexico. These explorers came from Spain. They tramped over mountains, plains, and deserts searching for mineral wealth. For some of the lucky ones their dreams came true.

Few countries of the world are so rich in mineral wealth as Mexico. Coal and oil are found along the slopes and coastal lowlands. Metal-producing minerals are found in the mountain and plateau areas.

In 1525 the great silver vein of Guanajuato was discovered. For four hundred years the mines of Guanajuato alone furnished from one fifth to two fifths of the silver in the entire world. More than one and a half billion dollars worth of silver has poured out of these fabulous mines. Even today Mexico produces more than half of the world's supply of silver.

Almost every mineral known to man is found in Mexico. In addition to silver, gold,

Mexican oil is refined at modern plants like this one at Salamanca, over a mile above sea level.

Mexican craftsmen are famous for their gaily-decorated pottery, like this huge jar at right.

copper, and iron ore, Mexico's mines produce lead, zinc, mercury, graphite, manganese, and many, many more.

Mining is Mexico's most important industry. But the Mexican people have benefited little from their country's mineral wealth. More than nine tenths of Mexico's mines are owned by people who live outside the country.

Mexico's oil is owned by the people of Mexico. All of the oil production is carried on by *Pemex,* a government-controlled company.

Oil was discovered in Mexico near Tampico in 1901. A few years later one of the greatest gushers ever known was struck. It produced 60,000 to 75,000 barrels of oil a day. So much oil flowed from the well that dirt reservoirs had to be hurriedly built to hold it. Today Mexico has some huge oil refineries. And near Mexico City gasoline is produced for use throughout the country.

Mexico has excellent possibilities for developing manufacturing. There are plenty of raw materials. For power resources, Mexico has a plentiful supply of oil, and some coal and water power.

But for many years there were few large or modern factories in Mexico. Most manufacturing was done in homes or small shops.

Leather goods, baskets, pottery, and silver jewelry—most of it produced in home workshops—remain important in Mexico. Nevertheless, changes are taking place.

New cotton mills have been built in the textile centers of Puebla and Orizaba. Monterrey, long the iron and steel center of Mexico, has added new blast furnaces. Many companies from the United States have built branch manufacturing plants in Mexico. These plants turn out machinery,

Mexican jewelry is a popular item with tourists. This jeweler is at work in his studio in Acapulco.

John Strohm

drugs, radios, chemicals, and a great variety of other manufactured products. Most of these new plants are located in Mexico City.

Mexico is still importing many manufactured goods. But it is working hard to become less dependent on outside sources. More than three fourths of Mexico's imports come from the United States. And, in return, nearly three fourths of Mexico's exports are shipped to the United States.

David Forbert—Shostal

Herbert Lanks—Gendreau

William Neil Smith

Herbert Lanks—Gendreau

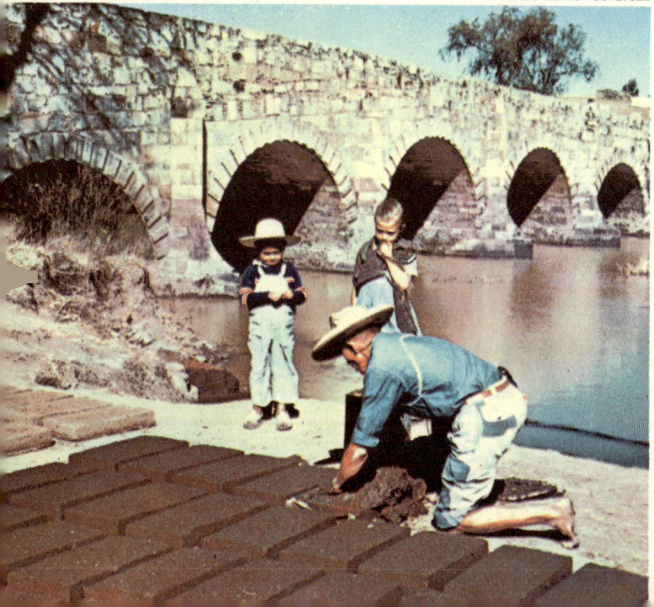

Village Life in Mexico

How do the people of Mexico live outside of Mexico City and the other large cities? What kind of homes do they have? How do they use their land? What foods do they eat? And what kind of clothes do they wear?

To find the answers to these questions, imagine that you have gone to visit a Mexican farm village. This village is in the highlands, not far from Mexico City. Most of the people of Mexico live in this central highland. And two thirds of Mexico's people are farmers. Here is what you would see.

About 100 houses cluster around an open square. This square is called a *plaza*. It is no easy job to count each house for they are close together, and in front of them is a high wall. The only clues that there are houses behind the wall are the doors that open onto small courtyards. These courtyards are a part of nearly all Mexican homes.

The wall and the houses are made of *adobe*. *Adobe* is a Spanish word meaning sun-dried brick. The *adobe* walls are thick. They keep the houses cool in summer and they keep out the cold wind in winter.

The houses are simple. Many have only one room. It is the living room and the bedroom for the entire family. Few of the houses have windows. There is only the door to let in light and fresh air.

Nearly all Mexican farmers live in villages. Indian farmers before the coming of the Spaniards also lived in villages. During Indian times all of the cropland belonged to the tribe. No individual owned land.

When the Spanish conquered Mexico, they took the land away from the tribes.

Traditional ways of life change slowly in Mexican villages like the one at top left.

A Tarahumara Indian girl (center) grinds corn into flour with her *metate* and rubbing stone.

An adobe brick-maker plies his ancient craft at Valle de Guadalupe in central Mexico (bottom).

The king of Spain then gave this land to his followers. In this way a few thousand Spaniards soon owned almost all of Mexico's cropland.

These large estates became known as *haciendas*. *Hacienda* is a Spanish word which means a large farm, worked by tenants and laborers instead of by the owner.

Most farm villages used to be part of *haciendas*. But a few years ago the Mexican government began to buy the large *haciendas*. The government then gave this land back to the Mexican farmers.

Today, in some farm villages, the people work the land together. They share the work of plowing, planting, and harvesting, and they also share the profits. In other farm villages, each farmer has his own fields which he works himself. In all of the farm villages the Mexican government is trying to help the farmers by showing them how to grow better crops by using good seed and fertilizer.

Jane Latta

Colorful piles of fruits and vegetables are displayed at the weekly market in Taxco.

Mexican women do their washing at the community laundry as a farmer hoes his corn in the background. Corn is Mexico's chief food crop.

Ray Manley—Shostal

This irrigation project at Culiacán, in western Mexico, provides water for a booming farming region.

Tortillas and *frijoles* — corn pancakes and beans—tell the story of food. Corn is Mexico's most important food. Indian farmers grew corn long before the Spaniards arrived, and it is still grown on more than two thirds of Mexico's cropland.

Beans are important to Mexicans too. Beans are Mexico's second most important food crop. They are valued because they are rich in protein. Many people get their protein from meat. But most Mexican farmers

Indian fishermen of Lake Patzcuaro are famous for their butterfly-shaped nets.

are too poor to afford much meat. So beans usually take the place of meat in Mexican meals.

Mexican cowboys, like cowboys in the United States and Canada, like broad-brimmed hats. The Mexican calls his hat a *sombrero*. The *sombrero* is worn by Mexican farmers as well as by cowboys.

A *sombrero* protects the farmer and the cowboy from the hot sun and the rain. Having a *sombrero* is like having an extra pocket. Mexicans use the curled-up brims of their *sombreros* to carry things.

Mexican farmers wear cotton clothing. Almost all of this clothing is made at home. Men and boys wear loose-fitting white trousers and shirts. Women and girls wear white blouses and gaily colored skirts.

Because it gets cold in the highlands in winter, and after the sun has set at night, cotton clothing is not warm enough. The women wrap shawls over their heads and shoulders. *Serapes* keep the men and boys warm. A *serape* is a hand-woven blanket. It has a slit in the center. The farmer puts his head through the slit and drapes the *serape* over him. As the sun gets higher in the sky, and the day becomes warmer, the farmer removes his *serape*. He folds it and slings it over his shoulder. At night when he goes to bed, the *serape* becomes the farmer's blanket.

If corn and beans are the main food crops, what else do Mexican farmers grow? First, it is important to know that Mexico has only a small amount of cropland. Much of Mexico is too rugged or too dry for farming. Less than one twentieth of Mexico's total land area is used for growing crops. But the great variety of landforms and climates in Mexico has given its farmers an opportunity to produce a variety of crops.

The dry northern portion of Mexico is ranch country. Some ranches are huge. In the olden days several ranches had more than a million acres.

Because the range is dry, many cattle are shipped to other parts of Mexico to be fattened before slaughtering. Most of the scrawny, tough range cattle are sold only for their hides and tallow. No one could chew the meat!

If you could fly over northern Mexico, here and there you would see patches of green on the brown desert below you. Green on the desert means that irrigation water is available. The government is busy building dams and reservoirs to increase Mexico's irrigated lands.

Mexico's largest irrigation project is called Laguna, a Spanish word meaning lake. The Laguna district is near the city of Torreón. More than half of the Laguna cropland is used for cotton, which is now Mexico's leading export.

Crops of central Mexico include wheat and corn in the cool highlands; coffee on the slopes; and bananas, sugar cane, and coconuts on the hot coastal plain. Each elevation has its own crops. This shows the effect of altitude on temperature.

From the Yucatan Peninsula come two important products. One is raised on plantations in the drier north. The other is

Otto Done—FPG

A Mexican laborer dressed in traditional white clothing spreads coffee berries to dry in the sun.

gathered in the dense rain forests to the south. The plantation crop is henequen. Its strong fibers are used in making binding cord. Years ago the entire world's supply of henequen fiber came from Yucatan, but today increasing amounts are being grown in East Africa. Mexican leaders are worried about the future of their henequen industry.

If you like to chew gum you should be interested in Yucatan's other product. It is chicle. Chicle puts the "chew" in chewing gum. It comes from the sap of the sapodilla tree which grows wild in the rain forests.

After drying on racks, henequen fibers are gathered into huge bales for export to world markets.

Robert Leahey—Shostal

CENTRAL AMERICA

COLOMBIA

JAMAICA

C A R I B B E A N   S E A

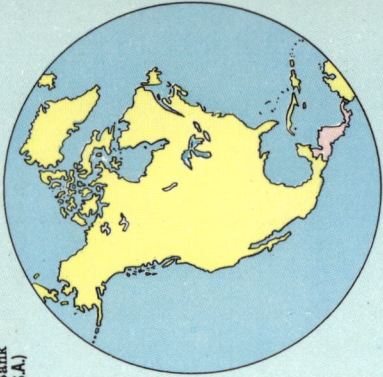

Serranilla Bank (Col. and U.S.A.)

Serrana Bank (Col. and U.S.A.)

Roncador Bank (Col. and U.S.A.)

Quita Sueño Bank (Col. and U.S.A.)

Old Providence I. (Col.)

St. Andrews I. (Col.)

Corn Islands (Nic. and U.S.A.)

Swan Islands (U.S.A.)

Cape Gracias a Dios

Patuca Point
Cape Camarón

Cape Blanco

SERRANÍA DEL DARIÉN
CORD. DE SAN BLAS
Chimán
La Palma
Garachiné
Jaqué
P A N A M A
Colón
Silver City
Panamá
Balboa
Pearl Is.
PANAMA CANAL ZONE (U.S.A.)
La Chorrera
Penonomé
Aguadulce
Chitré
Las Tablas
Río de Jesús
Santiago
Soná
SERRANÍA DE TABASARA
San Cristóbal
Mala Point
Azuero Peninsula
Gulf of Panama
Mosquito Gulf
Bocas del Toro
Chiriqui Lagoon
Chiriqui Gulf
David
Remedios
Horconcitos
Puerto Armuelles
Concepción
Coiba I.
Gulf of Chiriqui
Burica Point

COSTA RICA
CORD. DE TALAMANCA
Chirripó 11,410
Limón
Vesta
Suretka
Negrita
Alajuela
Heredia
San José
Cartago
Dominical
Osa Peninsula
Coronado Bay
CORDILLERA DE GUANACASTE
Santa Cruz
Nicoya
Nicoya Peninsula
Puntarenas
Papagayo Gulf
Gulf of Nicoya
San Juan del Norte
San Juan R.
San Carlos

NICARAGUA
MOSQUITO COAST
Prinzapolka
Puerto Cabezas
Bluefields
Rama
Escondido R.
Grande R.
Pearl Lagoon
Lake Nicaragua
Lake Managua
CORDILLERA ISABELA
Cape Gracias a Dios
Yablis
Cabezas
Bocay
Wawa R.
Tuma R.
Coco R.
San Rafael del Norte
Jinotega
Matagalpa
Juigalpa
Acoyapa
Managua
Masaya
Granada
Ometepe I.
Rivas
San Juan del Sur
Estelí
León
Chinandega
Nagarote
Diriamba
Jinotepe
Corinto

HONDURAS
Caratasca Lagoon
MTS.
Brewers
Aguán R.
Catacamas
Juticalpa
Patuca R.
Danlí
Ocotal
Trujillo
Tocoa
Sabá
Aguán
Roatán
Bay Islands
La Ceiba
Tela
Progreso
San Pedro Sula
Puerto Cortés
Ulúa R.
L. Yojoa
Comayagua
La Paz
Tegucigalpa
Yuscarán
Choluteca
Ponteloa
Gulf of Fonseca
San Francisco
San Miguel
La Unión

BRITISH HONDURAS
Corozal
Orange Walk
Belize
Stann Creek
Punta Gorda
Cayo
Benque Viejo
Turneffe I.
Ambergris Cay
Gulf of Honduras
Sarstún R.
Belize R.

GUATEMALA
SIERRA MADRE
Tajumulco - 13,316 ▲
MAYA MTS.
Piedras Negras
L. Petén
Flores
Dolores
Cobán
Livingston
Puerto Barrios
Gualán
Izabal
Motagua R.
Zacapa
Copán
Chiquimula
Santa Rosa de Copán
Ocotepeque
Metapán
Huehuetenango
Quezaltenango
Totonicapán
L. Atitlán
Sololá
Chimaltenango
Antigua Guatemala
Guatemala City
Escuintla
Jalapa
Jutiapa
Chalchuapa
San José
Mazatenango
Coatepeque
Retalhuleu
Ocós
Concepción
Usumacinta R.

EL SALVADOR
Santa Ana
Izalco - 6,184 ▲
Nueva San Salvador
San Salvador
Sonsonate
Zacatecoluca
Cojutepeque
San Vicente
Usulután
Lempa R.

M E X I C O

P A C I F I C   O C E A N

● National Capitals

Miles
0   50   100   200

San Salvador ─── 100,000-250,000 population
Tegucigalpa ─── 50,000-100,000 population
Alajuela ─── Under 50,000 population

© Copyright 1960 by Map Projects Inc.

CENTRAL AMERICA,
BRIDGE BETWEEN TWO CONTINENTS

A land bridge connects North and South America. South of Mexico this land bridge is called Central America. Six independent countries occupy this Central American land bridge. There is also a British colony. None of these countries, or the colony, is larger than a small state in the United States.

Start at the southern border of Mexico. Here is the way the countries of Central America are located as you travel south:

Guatemala	British Honduras
El Salvador	Honduras
Nicaragua	
Costa Rica	
	Panama

Christopher Columbus was the first European to sight Central America. He sailed along the coast of Honduras in 1502.

All of Central America came under the control of Spain. In 1821 Mexico and Central America broke away from Spain. For

David Forbert—Alpha

A modern highway winds through the Potrero Cerrado Valley of Costa Rica.

a short time all of the countries of Central America except Panama became a part of Mexico. But this did not last long. Central American leaders decided to form one large country, which they called the Federation of Central America.

Lake Atitlán, completely surrounded by volcanoes, is in the highlands of Guatemala.

David Forbert—Alpha

These women are taking great loads of flowers to a village market in Honduras.

David Forbert—Alpha

Pierre M. Martinot

Ruins of the ancient Mayan civilization are found in both Mexico and Guatemala. Where clearings are not maintained, the jungle completely hides the ruins.

But most of Central America is mountainous, and there are dense tropical forests on the lowlands along the coasts. It is still difficult to travel by land from country to country. During the time of the Federation, more than 100 years ago, it was almost impossible. When each country wanted its own independence, the government of the Federation could not hold the various parts of the region together. By 1842 the map of Central America looked as it does today.

Tortillas, made of ground corn, are a basic food. Girls learn how to make them at an early age.

John Strohm

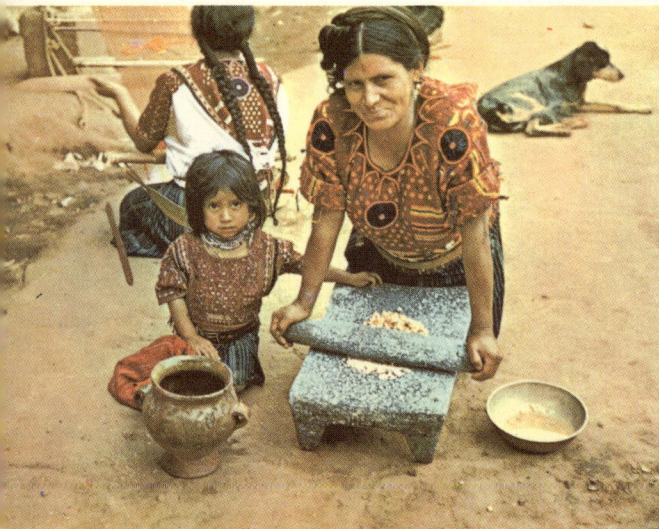

Guatemalan children in their classroom. There are not yet enough schools for all.

Tom Hollyman—Photo Researchers

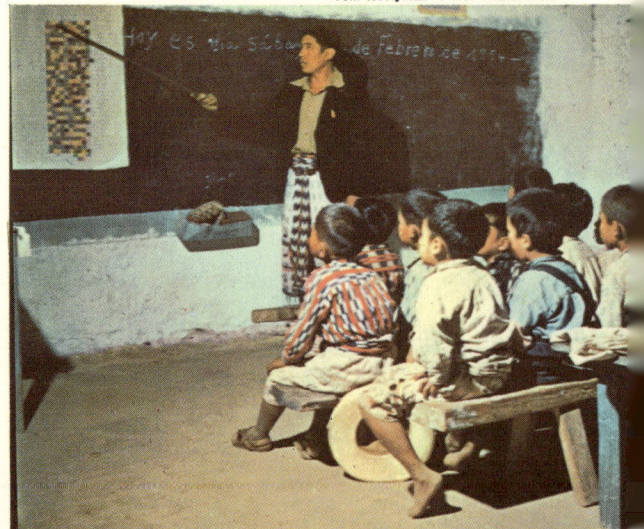

Many people in Central America have Indian ancestors. Guatemala is the most Indian of all the Central American countries. There, three fifths of the population are pure Indian. These Indians are descendants of the Mayans.

Some Central American Indians have kept the ways of their ancestors. They live in small villages. Each village has its own customs and beliefs, and even its own style of clothing. If you spend a great deal of time in Guatemala, you will come to learn what part of the highland an Indian comes from by his costume.

Indians look forward to market day. They travel for miles to the village that is holding a market. They carry pottery, cloth, and boxes of vegetables and chickens stacked high on their heads. They hope to sell these goods at the market. But the market is more than a place to buy and sell goods. It is also a place to meet friends and exchange gossip.

John Strohm

Chichicastenango is a famous Indian market village in the highlands of Guatemala.

Indians gather around a pottery seller in a Guatemalan market village.

Herbert Lanks—Shostal

Tropical Plantations —Coffee and Bananas

Central America is tropical. The lowlands are hot. So most of the people, nearly all of the important cities, and most of the roads, railroads, airports, and cropland are found in the highlands. In some of the countries more than three fourths of the people live in the highlands.

Coffee is the chief highland crop. It was first planted in Costa Rica more than 150 years ago. Today coffee is grown in all of the Central American countries except Panama. Central American coffee is noted for its fine flavor. Most of it is grown between 2,000 and 4,500 feet above the sea.

Careful picking of only the ripe berries makes Central American coffee especially valuable.

Plantations like this one in Costa Rica produce exceptionally fine-flavored coffee.

This is the "mountain grown coffee" that you hear about in radio and television commercials.

Men and nature work closely together in Central America to produce fine coffee. The men give their coffee trees special care. Coffee trees are often planted in the shade of taller trees. Shade-grown coffee has an especially delicious flavor.

Owners of coffee plantations see that harvesting is done carefully. At harvest time the trees are covered with coffee berries. Some berries are green, some are bright red, and some are dark red. Only the dark red berries are picked.

The coffee pickers return to the same tree over and over. Each time they pick only the ripe berries. This is slow work. But their careful efforts have made Central American coffee especially valuable.

Nature has helped, too. The soil in the coffee highlands is deep and rich. This soil has been made from volcanic ash. Volcanic ash produces the finest of all coffee soils.

The Central American coffee highlands have an ideal climate. They are high

These workmen are unloading a car of ripe coffee berries in El Salvador.

Spraying operations are carried on regularly to prevent the spread of banana diseases.

Courtesy of the United Fruit Company

enough so that it never gets very hot. Yet they are not so high that there is ever danger from frost. The 50 to 60 inches of rainfall and the dry harvest season are perfect for growing coffee.

While coffee rules the highlands, bananas dominate the lowlands. Bananas thrive on hot weather, and they like plenty of rainfall. Both are available in abundance in the Central American lowlands.

Growing bananas is big business. First the dense vegetation has to be cleared. Then engineers have to build drainage systems to keep the flat land from flooding. Railroad tracks must be laid throughout the plantation, and more tracks are laid to the port on the coast where the bananas are loaded on ships. Even towns have to be built to house the workers. Some banana plantations have thousands of workers.

A few years ago a serious disease almost ruined the Central American banana plantations. Some plantations were moved from the Caribbean coast to the Pacific coast in the hope that they might escape the disease, but it followed them.

Scientists finally saved the plantations. They discovered that they could control the disease by spraying the banana plants. Pipelines were quickly laid on the fields. These pipelines carry chemicals, which are sprayed on the banana plants every few days. The spraying must be repeated often, for the heavy rains of the lowlands soon wash off the chemicals.

Bananas are picked while green to prevent their spoiling before reaching northern markets.

Courtesy of the United Fruit Company

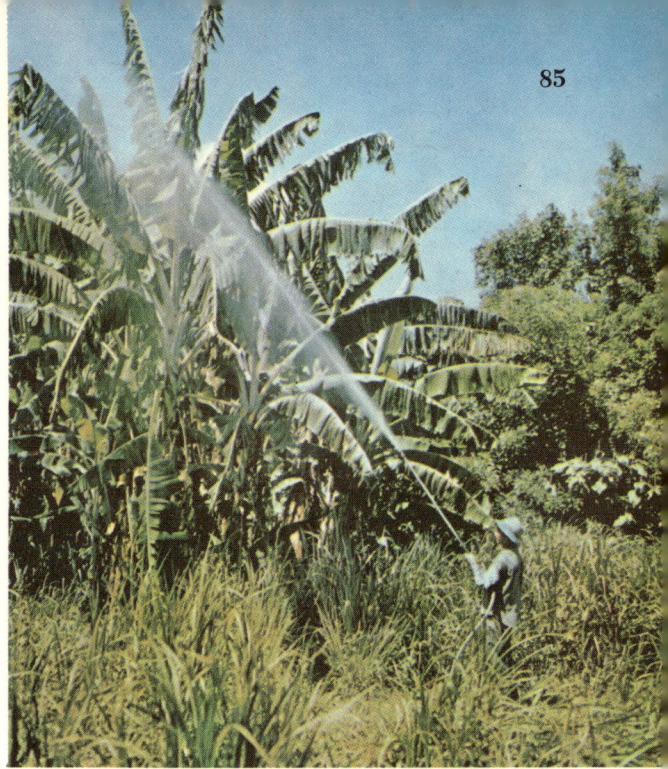

Bananas make up more than three fifths of the total value of Panama's exports.

Courtesy of the United Fruit Company

This ship is sailing through the Gaillard Cut, one of the highest points on the Panama Canal.

The Panama Canal

The Panama Canal was opened to ships less than 50 years ago. But how important it has become! Think of a ship sailing from New York to Hawaii. Before the canal was built, it took weeks of extra time and thousands of extra miles to make the long trip around South America.

The United States controls a strip of land five miles on either side of the canal. This strip of land is called the Canal Zone. It cuts across the center of the country of Panama. The United States pays Panama a yearly rent for use of the Canal Zone.

The Panama Canal is one of the world's great engineering projects. At its highest point, Gatun Lake, the canal is 85 feet above sea level. To raise ships to this height and bring them back down again, huge locks were built.

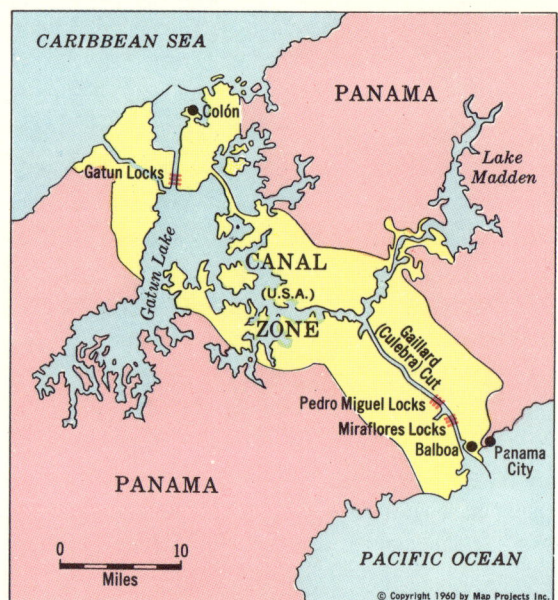

When a ship moves into a lock, a gate is closed behind it. Then water is pumped into the lock. In this way the level of the water, and the ship, is raised. When the ship leaves this lock it is at the level of the next lock. In this way it finally reaches Gatun Lake. Then, another series of locks lowers the ship to sea level.

It takes a ship seven to eight hours to pass through the canal. In some years more than 8,000 large commercial ships use the canal. In addition, many small vessels, as well as Navy ships, make use of this short-cut from ocean to ocean.

The Miraflores Locks lower ships from the Gaillard Cut to the Pacific Ocean.

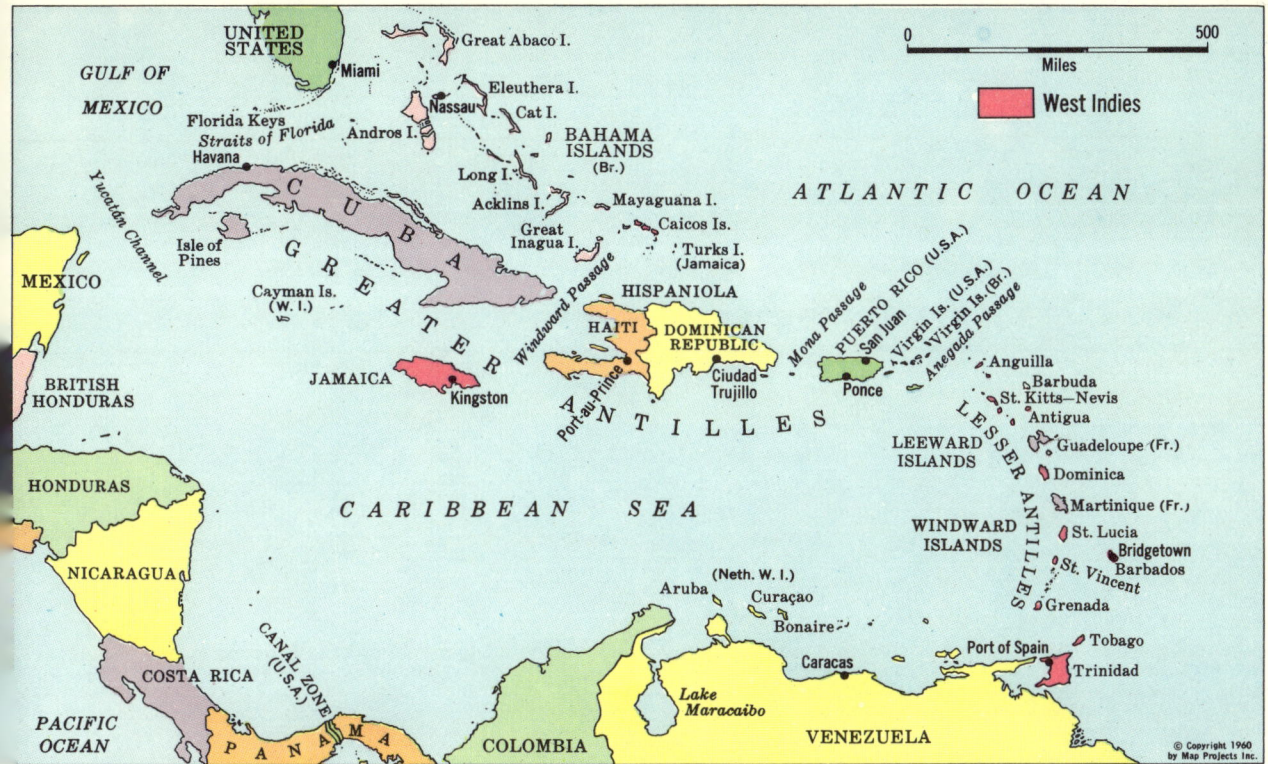

THE CARIBBEAN ISLANDS

To the east of the Yucatan Peninsula and Central America, between North and South America, is a vast expanse of water. This is the Caribbean Sea. In a great curve across the Caribbean, from Florida to the northern coast of South America, is a chain of islands. We call them the Caribbean islands.

These Caribbean islands are the tops of mountain ranges that rise above the sea. Some are as large as an average sized state in the United States, but others are no bigger than a city lot.

People live on more than 50 of the Caribbean islands. But there are thousands of tiny islands, rocks, and reefs that are too small to support human life.

Many flags fly over the islands of the Caribbean Sea. Among the islands there are three independent countries — Cuba, Haiti, and the Dominican Republic.

Passengers wait for a bus in Haiti, part of the Caribbean island of Hispaniola.

Fritz Henle—Photo Researchers

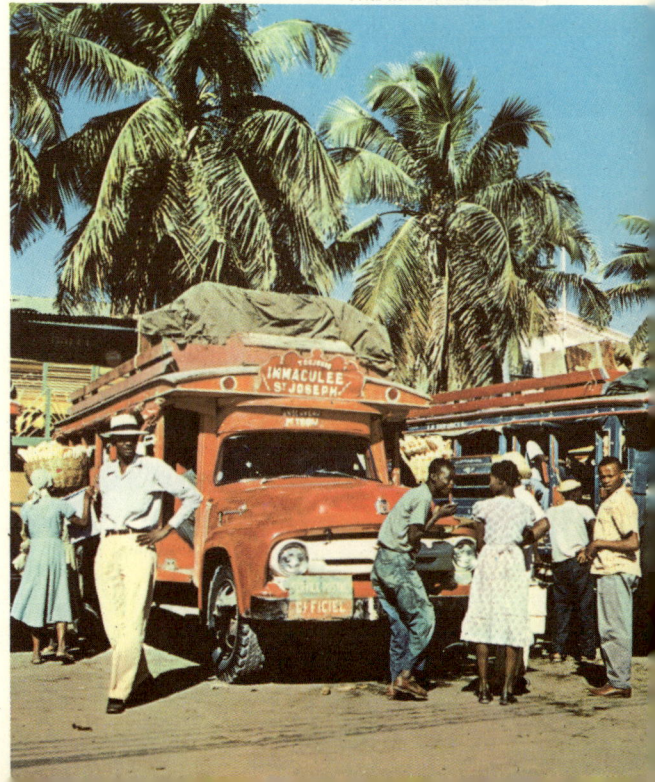

Here is the sheltered harbor of St. George's, the chief port and trading center of Grenada. The island, discovered by Christopher Columbus, is covered by rugged, forested mountains.

There are also two self-governing commonwealths. One is the Commonwealth of Puerto Rico, which is associated with the United States. The other is the British Caribbean Federation. It is best known as The West Indies. Trinidad is its capital. All of the British islands in the Caribbean, except the Bahamas and the British Virgin Islands, are members of the Federation.

In addition to all of these, the flags of the United States, France, the Netherlands, and Venezuela fly over islands in the Caribbean Sea.

The Caribbean islands have a truly "temperate" climate. The islands are bathed by warm ocean currents. Gentle trade winds blow in off the open ocean.

Trade winds blow from the northeast. As the air blows in off the ocean it strikes the northern and eastern slopes of the mountains. The air is forced to rise to get over the mountains. As it rises, the air begins to cool. Rain falls from this cooled air.

The windward sides of the islands, those sides that face the wind, are wet. The leeward sides, those facing away from the wind, are often quite dry. San Juan, on the windward coast of Puerto Rico, receives over 60 inches of rain each year. Ponce, on the leeward coast, receives only 36 inches. Some of the highest islands get soaked. On the windward side of the Blue Mountains in Jamaica one weather station receives an average of 222 inches of rain each year. Yet at Kingston, just 30 miles away on the leeward side of Jamaica, the average yearly rainfall is only about 29 inches.

On the eastern side of the islands the trade winds bring high waves on shore. This made it dangerous for sailing ships in the early days. The western sides of the islands afforded safer anchorages. For this reason almost all of the chief towns on the islands are on the leeward sides.

Many countries have interests in the Caribbean islands. The people of these islands have come from every part of the world. People of all races live on the islands. Nevertheless, the ways of living are similar throughout the Caribbean.

The Caribbean islands are in the tropics. Days throughout the year are warm. The year-round average temperature in Havana, for example, is 77 degrees. There is little difference in temperature from winter to summer. At Bridgetown, in Barbados, there is a difference of only four degrees between the warmest and the coldest months of the year.

This tropical climate makes it possible for the islanders to grow highly valuable, warmth-loving plants. Sugar cane ranks at the top of the list of these tropical plants in the Caribbean. On almost every island where there is any farming at all, some sugar cane is sure to be grown, and to some islands, no crop could be more important. Cuba is sometimes called a giant sugar bowl.

St. Lucia, a beautiful tropical island, is a member of the British Caribbean Federation. Its fertile valleys and narrow coastal plains are mainly used in producing sugar cane, St. Lucia's chief product.

Courtesy of Pan American World Airways

Fritz Henle—Photo Researchers

These men, on St. Lucia, are hollowing logs to be used for fishing canoes.

The catch taken by these Grenada fishermen will be sold fresh in local markets.

George Leavens—Photo Researchers

The real contrasts in ways of living are not from island to island, but between the lowlands and the highlands on each island.

The lowlands are densely settled. Only those places on the leeward sides of islands that are too dry for farming have few people. The natural landscape of the lowlands has been completely changed by man. Forests have been cleared, brushland has been burned over time after time, and grasslands have been plowed. This land has been changed so that crops could be planted and cities, towns, and villages could be built.

The choicest portions of the lowlands are usually reserved for sugar cane. Much of this land is owned by large sugar companies or by wealthy planters.

Farmers who live on the plantations plant the cane in the early spring. But they do not have to replant each year, for

Courtesy of the Puerto Rico News Service

Huge fields of sugar cane occupy Puerto Rico's fertile valleys.

Much of the hard work of cutting sugar cane is still done by hand in Cuba.

Courtesy of the United Fruit Company

new plants will grow from the stalks of old sugar cane. Some plantations use machinery to plant and to cultivate the sugar cane land. But on most of the islands the work is still done by hand.

The summer and autumn months are spent cultivating the cane. Only a few workers are needed for this job. Many people in the islands find it difficult to get work in the summer and fall months and the unemployment rate is high.

But the harvest season is a different story. From December to June thousands of workers are needed in the cane fields. At that time of year no one has trouble finding a job. The cane is cut by hand. It is then quickly carried to the mill in ox-carts, trucks, or railroad cars. At the mill the cane is cut into pieces, which are then crushed by huge rollers to squeeze out the juice. Finally the juice is boiled until it forms hard crystals of sugar.

Courtesy of the Puerto Rico News Service

Most island farms grow bananas for home use. Bananas for export are grown on plantations.

Courtesy of the Puerto Rico News Service

Mangoes are a favorite fruit in the Caribbean. They are also exported to the United States.

George Leavens—Photo Researchers

Although sugar cane is by far the most important crop of the lowlands, many other crops are grown. Some of these are pineapples, winter-grown vegetables, coconuts, citrus fruits, cacao, and bananas. Most of these crops are exported to the United States and Canada, or across the Atlantic to Europe.

The way of life is quite different in the highlands of the Caribbean islands. Because slopes in the highlands are generally steep, and the soil is often thin, there are few areas where large-scale farming is found.

In some few places, particularly western Cuba, Haiti, interior Puerto Rico, and eastern Jamaica, special highland crops such as coffee and tobacco are grown. But in most parts of the highlands, there are no signs of plantation farming.

These women, in the highlands of Grenada, are preparing coffee berries for drying. The berries must be carefully dried to ensure a good flavor.

The highlands are thinly settled. Farmers who live in the highlands grow only subsistence crops. This means that they grow crops for their own use, rather than to sell. Patches of bananas, corn, yams, beans, and squash can be seen clinging to mountain slopes.

Because the slopes are so steep, it is impossible to use farm machinery in the highlands. All of the work of clearing the land, plowing, and cultivating is done by hand. Great care must be taken to keep the soil from washing away.

Tiny villages of crude huts huddle together in narrow mountain valleys, or even on the steep slopes of the mountains themselves. Few real roads lead into the heart of the island mountain country. Only narrow trails wind through the forests and over the ridges. Such trails are meant for mules or burros, not for automobiles.

Courtesy of the Puerto Rico News Service

Above, many Puerto Rican farmers use tiny hillside patches like this one to produce tobacco.

Space for houses is limited in the mountainous regions of the Caribbean islands (below).

Slide Library—American Museum of Natural History

NORTH AMERICA'S FUTURE

It was just a little over 450 years ago that Christopher Columbus and his men sailed their ships into the waters off the North American continent. At that time the world did not even know that North America existed.

Think of all that has happened in those 450 years. But what of the years that are yet to come?

The people of the countries of the northern two thirds of the continent, Canada and the United States, have much in common. The climate and landforms of southern Canada, where most Canadians live, and of the northern United States, where most Americans live, are similar. The ways of earning a living, the language, and the customs of these two countries are much alike. Neither the Canadian nor the citizen of the United States is considered a foreigner in the other's country. These are things that will not change.

Friendly co-operation between Canada and the United States will be essential for

A great network of new super-highways will link the people of North America more closely.

the future welfare of each. The St. Lawrence Seaway is one example of recent cooperation. The co-operative development of the northland, shared by both countries, is essential too. This is a region of great strategic importance. The defense of the entire North American continent depends upon the watchfulness of military outposts in the northlands.

What of Mexico, Central America, and the Caribbean islands? They seem different from the countries that lie to the north.

The St. Lawrence Seaway is opening a new sea lane from the ocean to the interior of the continent.

Languages, customs, foods, and ways of living are unfamiliar to people from Canada and the United States. Yet the lives of the people of these more southern lands are tied closely with the lives of their neighbors to the north.

Much of the exports of Mexico, Central America, and the Caribbean islands will continue to move northward. In return, goods from Canada and the United States will flow southward, as before.

The people of all of North America will feel closer in the future. This closeness will involve more than just trade. Trade goods are not the only things that cross borders between countries. Ideas travel too.

Art, music, books, movies, inventions, and knowledge of all kinds are the kind of ideas that can travel. There will be a greater exchange of these "ideas" in the future. People will be able to travel faster, farther, and more often in the years to come. The exchange of goods, people, and ideas will surely do much to bind more closely together all of the people who share the North American continent.

This Thor-Able rocket is emblematic of a new age of scientific discovery and exploration. Soon man will be able to travel in outer space.

This Bevatron is a vital key in atomic research.

Education for all North American boys and girls is the promise of the continent's future. Someday education will be available to everyone.

NORTH AMERICA — FACTS AND FIGURES

COUNTRIES: AREA AND POPULATION

Country	Area in sq. miles	Population (est. 1960)
Canada	3,851,113	17,606,000
U.S.A.	3,557,098	181,306,000
Mexico	760,373	34,530,000
Nicaragua	57,145	1,458,000
Cuba	44,206	6,727,000
Honduras	43,227	1,928,000
Guatemala	42,042	3,689,000
Panama	28,571	1,061,000
Costa Rica	23,421	1,138,000
Dominican Republic	19,333	2,989,000
Haiti	10,714	3,590,000
British Honduras	8,867	94,000
El Salvador	8,259	2,562,000

LARGE CITIES AND THEIR POPULATION

City and Country (or State)	Population (est. 1960)
New York, New York	7,886,900
Chicago, Illinois	3,811,400
Mexico City, Mexico	3,301,760
Los Angeles, California	2,472,000
Philadelphia, Pennsylvania	2,183,500
Detroit, Michigan	1,914,900
Baltimore, Maryland	1,455,400
Montreal, Canada	1,172,000
Cleveland, Ohio	952,700
Houston, Texas	950,000
Havana, Cuba	900,000
St. Louis, Missouri	870,100
Washington, D.C.	830,000
San Francisco, California	790,700
Milwaukee, Wisconsin	765,900
Boston, Massachusetts	743,000
Pittsburgh, Pennsylvania	686,600
Toronto, Canada	685,000

HIGHEST MOUNTAINS AND THEIR ELEVATIONS

Mountain and Country (or State)	Height in feet
McKinley, Alaska	20,270
Logan, Canada	19,850
Orizaba, Mexico	18,700
St. Elias, Alaska-Canada	18,008
Popocatepetl, Mexico	17,887
Ixtacihuatl, Mexico	17,342
Foraker, Alaska	17,280
Lucania, Canada	17,150
King, Canada	17,130
Steele, Canada	16,439
Bona, Alaska	16,420
Sanford, Alaska	16,208
Blackburn, Alaska	16,140
Wood, Canada	15,880
Whitney, California (21st in size)	14,495

LARGEST LAKES AND THEIR AREAS

Lake and Country	Area in sq. miles
Superior, Canada-U.S.A.	31,820
Huron, Canada-U.S.A.	23,010
Michigan, U.S.A.	22,400
Great Bear, Canada	12,000
Great Slave, Canada	11,170
Erie, Canada-U.S.A.	9,940
Winnipeg, Canada	9,398
Ontario, Canada-U.S.A.	7,540
Nicaragua, Nicaragua	3,100
Athabaska, Canada	3,058
Winnipegosis, Canada	2,086
Manitoba, Canada	1,817

LONGEST RIVERS AND THEIR LENGTH

River and Country	Length in miles
Missouri, U.S.A.	2,714
Mackenzie, Canada	2,514
Mississippi, U.S.A.	2,350
St. Lawrence, Canada-U.S.A.	2,350
Yukon, Canada-U.S.A.	1,979
Rio Grande, U.S.A.-Mexico	1,800
Arkansas, U.S.A.	1,450
Colorado, U.S.A.-Mexico	1,400
Ohio, U.S.A.	1,306
Red, U.S.A.	1,300
Saskatchewan, Canada	1,205
Columbia, U.S.A.	1,200
Peace, Canada	1,054
Snake, U.S.A.	1,038